Carry Me Back

An American Journey in Time and Place

By Arthur Pope

Copyright © 2015 Arthur Pope
All rights reserved.

ISBN: 1511692308
ISBN 13: 9781511692304

Library of Congress Control Number: 2015905788
Createspace Independent Publishing Platform
North Charleston, South Carolina

Dedication

For my children

Sarah Rebecca Pope
Ethan Josiah Pope

Certain places seem to exist mainly because someone has written about them. A place belongs forever to whoever claims it hardest, remembers it most obsessively, wrenches it from itself, shapes it, renders it, loves it so radically that he remakes it in his own image.

Joan Didion
The White Album

Introduction

This is a book about seeking ancestry and about the bond and mystery of time and place. For over fifty years, I have been engaged in a love affair with the legends surrounding my family history as it unfolded in the 19th and early 20th centuries in Berryville, Clarke County, Virginia. As a child growing up in an idyllic neighborhood in New Haven, Connecticut, during the early 1950s, I was beguiled by these legends filled with emotional tales of landscape, tradition and people.

To heighten my interest, there was an old trunk in our attic that had been shipped North in the 1930s when the last immediate family members to live in Berryville died. The trunk was filled with photographs and memorabilia of Clarke County, Virginia, the antebellum South, the Confederacy, Methodism, and American small town southern life.

As I grew older and moved beyond the mysteries and emotions that all of this evoked, many other questions began to arise such as how my family dealt with the larger issues of slavery and American apartheid. I began to ask what it was that they, as Confederates and Methodists, actually believed and how did their circumstances parallel American history itself. Thus began a 50 year search to rediscover these people, the time and place in which they lived, and what that place is like today. This book is their story.

Fifty years out from the New Haven neighborhood where my tale begins, an afterword details how time transformed that charmed neighborhood into one of the most dangerous and crime ridden in the state, offering yet another example of the evolution of American place.

Over the years, I was to learn that my own family history was really a prototype of American history and that we are all connected to our past in a myriad of ways that decades cannot erase. Sometimes memories get twisted and sometimes the past is elusive. But to live again in its enclosure can be one of the most enriching and enlightening experiences that life has to offer.

Arthur Pope

1

New Haven, Connecticut
Early 1950s

I grew up in a two family house on oak lined Bassett Street in New Haven, Connecticut. The house, of colonial revival style had been built fifty years earlier on land that was basically woods and swamp with views of Farnum's, a large farm that sat below West Rock, one of two ancient basalt cliffs that dominate the New Haven skyline. In the 1950s New Haven was a city of about 160,000 residents and most noted for the presence of the font of intellectualism, Yale University, the Winchester Repeating Arms Company, and the manufacture of carriages, clocks and locks.

Bassett Street, on the upper end, was crossed by Newhall Street which contained a small-town-like commercial district known as Newhallville. In essence, we lived in a small town within a large city and frequently roamed the significant remnants of a rural farm. At one of its borders the farm sat on a body of water that we knew as the Lagoon and which flowed into a creek where the Civilian Conservation Corps had developed a swimming hole in the 1930s.

It was a wonderful world to grow up in for me, my two brothers and our sister. In addition to the farm, we had within walking distance the Peabody Museum and the New Haven Historical Society. These institutions reinforced our love for the place in which we lived. Other places like the New Haven Green, Savin Rock Amusement Park (the Coney Island of New England), Lighthouse Point Park, and our neighborhood churches and schools contributed to give us a somewhat charmed childhood on which to look back.

Our early education was provincial indeed and took place at the Abraham Lincoln Grammar School, to which we walked along railroad tracks that ran parallel to the remnants of the early 19th century Farmington Canal. It was an anachronistic world that was to completely vanish within a few short years.

Our teachers were mostly unmarried older women. They were the same women who, in many cases, had taught our parents. According to our teachers, there were two great presidents - George Washington (whose reproduced Gilbert Stuart portrait hung on each classroom wall together with a key-wound New Haven Clock Company school clock) and Abraham Lincoln who, of course, "freed the slaves" and whose large, gloomy reproduced portrait dominated the dimly lit second floor corridor of the school. Most of what we knew about slavery we learned from books like *Uncle Tom's Cabin*.

There were two great wars to learn about, the American Revolution and the Civil War. As to the latter, only Northern history was taught. The South consisted mainly of slave owning villains who were largely suspect, with the exception of Stonewall Jackson and Robert E. Lee who were considered misguided footnotes on the list of American heroes.

I remember that my sixth grade history text book ended before World War I. Strange, as we often times rehearsed "duck and cover" tactics in case the Russians zapped us with an atom bomb. The most important subject was penmanship and all our writing was done with pens dipped in inkwells on our desks. Psalms 1 and 23 and the poem "Columbus" were memorized. We had a wind up phonograph located in the back of the classroom, an area that was lined on three sides with blackboards. The remaining side had large windows looking out into the tops of huge elm trees. We sang a lot. Songs like "The Arkansas Traveler," "Down in the Valley" and "Long, Long Ago".

Suffice it to say, this was our world. It was a world that captivated us, and it was a world we loved. It was the only world we knew. Except, that is, for one other legendary place that had been infused in our minds and hearts - Berryville, Virginia.

My maternal grandparents, Adolph and Augusta Konopacke, were Eastern European immigrants who came to this country early in the 20th Century. My grandfather was a modest success story who bought and sold real estate, mostly in Newhallville. While the Konopackes did tell us some stories about growing up in the old country, they always seemed to have more fondness for their exuberant lives in the new world.

My paternal grandparents were a different story. My grandmother, Minnie Fields Pope, constantly enchanted us with stories and legends of her wonderful, complex New Haven background that included descent from Mayflower passengers, John Davenport, the founder of New Haven, and numerous American Revolutionaries. She told us of her father's experience as a drummer boy in the Civil War and strange tales of Yankee decadence including drunken binges and illegal prize fights on fishing barges in Long Island Sound. My grandfather, Arthur Townsend Pope, who died when I was a year old, was born and raised in Berryville, Virginia. I suppose that should have been that. But it wasn't.

Over the years my grandmother, my father, Warren Lee Pope, and my uncle, Arthur (Art) Townsend Pope Jr., conveyed to us, with great gusto and emotion, stories about this town *down South*. There were tales about our great grandfather, John Michael Pope, a Confederate soldier cited for distinguished service who was so taken with Robert E. Lee that he promised him that his children and theirs would carry on his name for generations (they have). We were also told reverent tales of Stonewall Jackson to whose brigade John Michael belonged.

There were stories of people and places in Berryville that included the beautiful Esther Lee, my great grandfather's first born. There were tales of my great aunt Ursula Virginia (known as Jennie) who worked in a place called Coiners Department store in Berryville, and her sister, Hannah Showers Pope, who married George Cunningham, a revered Methodist layman and supervisor of the Berryville Mills. We were told again and again of how the entire town of Berryville shut down on the day of Cunningham's funeral. We were told that life was *different* down south, that folks were much more friendly and life more romantic. At least, in retrospect, I think that is what they were trying to convey.

All of this seemed to get summed up during family "sing alongs" when, in an almost worshipful way, my grandmother Minnie (who had been to Berryville just once) looked toward heaven and accompanied my father on the piano as he rendered a slightly tearful and most soulful rendition of "Carry Me Back To Old Virginia." While my father had never been to Berryville, his father had obviously done a magnificent job of teaching him to love it.

To fuel the fire of enchantment, there was an old trunk in the attic of the house on Bassett Street that had been shipped to New Haven from the Methodist Home in Gaithsburg, Maryland, following the deaths, three months apart, of my grandfather's two sisters, Ursula Virginia and Hannah Showers. Both being frail, they had moved to the Home to live out their final days there in the 1930s.

Among the fascinating treasures in that trunk were a family Bible, a Renaissance Revival mantel clock, tinted prints of Robert E. Lee and Stonewall Jackson, and a porcelain covered photo album of numerous personages in Berryville, mostly unidentified. One of the photographs was an intriguing portrait of a stately woman dressed with American Indian accessories and drawing a bow and arrow. We wondered who could she possibly be?

There were award books presented by Berryville High School for scholarship and deportment, letters, numerous hymn books from the Methodist Episcopal Church South with the pages of favorite hymns stained by oil from the hands of those who had held and turned them many times. In some ways the trunk presented more mystery than insight, but it helped to sear Berryville into our imaginative lives. If there were truly such a thing as genetic memory, we were seized by it.

Map of Newhallville. West Rock and Farnum's Farm were to the upper left. Abraham Lincoln School was on the corner of Shelton and Division Streets. The former railway and Farmington Canal are between Dixwell Avenue and Newhall Street.

Early 20th century photo of Farnum's Farm. Even by the late 1940s this scene had not changed that much. The Newhallville Neighborhood was to the west.
(Photo courtesy of Colin M. Caplan Magrissoforte.com)

The Abraham Lincoln Grammar School, New Haven, CT, as it appeared in the early 1960s.

Cover of the photograph album in the trunk in the attic in New Haven.

Unidentified photograph in the album. We always knew there must be quite a story there.

Bassett Street today looking towards West Rock, author's childhood home lower left. (National Register Photo courtesy Colin M. Caplan Magrissoforte.com.)

2

THE JOURNEY BEGINS

Following graduation from high school in 1961, my lively interest in American history and journalism continued to grow. I was entering college to pursue careers in these areas and, within the year, was to publish several local history articles. I must have had a lot of time on my hands that summer because Berryville began to loom large. Who were these people in the photographs? Were the stories true? Why was the whole thing so emotional?

There were also many other questions. Were we of English descent as our name implied? Who were our great great grandparents and how did they come to live in Berryville?

Questions about the family's religious devotion and adherence to the Methodist Episcopal Church South also interested me, as did my great grandfather's Civil War record and his strong idolization of Robert E. Lee and Stonewall Jackson.

Our family's views on slavery and race were of particular interest as this was a time in our country dominated by the civil rights movement. One of my closest black friends, Harris Hampton who, incidentally, was from Virginia, was impressing me with lectures on black history and his enchantment with W. E. B. Dubois. It was not exactly a good time to have "Confederates in the Attic".[1] But this all, nevertheless, increased my curiosity.

On top of it all there were still the many questions raised by the contents of that trunk in the attic such as who was the woman photographed in Native American attire? And so, at that young age, I found myself inquiring about my family by letter to Esta C. Brown, Secretary of the Town of Berryville. I do not have a record of what I asked about specifically, but I received an extensive letter in reply in June of 1962.

I was told that Mr. and Mrs. (Hannah Pope) George Cunningham and Miss Jennie Pope had lived on Main Street and that Mrs. Frank Hart (Esther) had lived in the adjacent property and still lived there. The letter confirmed that the family had been active in the Methodist Church and that Miss Jennie had indeed been employed at Coiner's Department store. I was even sent the address of a gentleman who had been her fellow employee and still worked at the store. Brown also provided me with the addresses of possible relatives living in town.

Far more importantly, I was sent the names and addresses of people who had known our family and were still living, including E.G. Coiner and 93 year old Nora Forester

Hardesty who, together with her daughter, Muriel Gregory, were to become good pen pal friends and shed much light on my family's history.

In response to my subsequent inquiries, Nora and Muriel spent quite a bit of time visiting folks in Berryville. They wrote me about a graveyard on the edge of town at a church called Stone's Chapel where they had located the graves of Michael Pope, brother of my great grandfather, John Michael, and another brother, Conrad, neither of whom we had ever heard mentioned. They also told of a sister, Barbara. All of these siblings, they said, had come from Germany as children and young adults.

I sent Nora and Muriel the photographs from the trunk in the attic, many of which they were able to identify. The woman in Native American garb was identified as Mrs. Province McCormick, wife of an Indian Inspector. I knew there had to be a larger story here, but was still a bit in the dark. Another important remembrance was that John Michael was raised by Hannah and Manuel Showers who lived on Main Street in the residence which, in modern times, had become the Battletown Inn.

After a year of correspondence, I put the project on hold for nearly a decade as I finished college and graduate school, married and developed my careers as minister, historic preservationist, social activist and freelance journalist.

3

THAT FIRST SICK HAPPY UNEASY BUT THRILLED FEELING

Raymond Lane, formerly with the Washington Post and the Wall Street Journal, writing in AARP Magazine tells about going to Ireland to trace his ancestry. He says there are studies out there that suggest we're all born with genetic memories – that we move through time carrying the experiences and cultures of our ancestors. He writes "The first time I saw Dublin I was filled with a kind of sick happy uneasy but thrilled feeling." [1] That is exactly what I felt on my first trip to Berryville with my wife, Esther, in the summer of 1971.

These feelings almost overwhelmed me as we drove by the hills and farms along Route 7 into the bustling little town of Berryville. We passed a number of pleasant old homes, an old inn and a number of churches before spotting the storied icon of family legend, Coiner's Department Store. We parked across the street in front of the town offices and, armed with my ten-year-old letters, went inside to see if we could get some directions and some more information.

We were met inside by some very friendly folk including John Enders, who we understood to be the local funeral director. We quickly learned that he and his wife "Dolly" owned and occupied the Pope family homestead on West Main Street.

After a long conversation with him, we went across the street into Coiner's Department Store which we discovered hadn't changed much since my great aunt Virginia worked there (1898 – 1922). We saw the same old cash and carry wire system from the second floor Bookkeeping Department and the same counters and desk where Aunt Jennie had worked. One of the present clerks related that, though she did not know Jennie, she "often heard tell of her." We learned that Mr. Coiner had died a couple of weeks earlier. He had been well into his 90s.

From Coiner's we went to the Pope home on quiet tree lined West Main Street. I called up to a lady washing the second floor windows (Dolly Enders) and when I asked if my forebears, the Popes, had lived there she replied "Oh my, this is it! I'll be right down." Within a few minutes we were seated in the living room as she told us the history of the house.

Next we went next door to see Dolly's mother, Esther S. Hart (granddaughter of my great grandfather's sister, Barbara Pope Greenwald). She had been named for my great aunt, Esther Lee Pope. We felt a bit like visiting royalty. Esther Hart knew our relatives intimately having lived next door to them for many years.

She told us many stories about my great grandfather, John Michael Pope, and his work as a tailor in town and about Hannah Pope and Jennie (Mrs. George Cunningham), children of my great grandfather and his wife, Harriet Hamilton Pope. Mrs. Hart still had my letter of ten years previous on her desk. Her affection for our family was obvious as she related how each Memorial Day she still placed flowers on the family grave site at the Green Hill Cemetery. She even remembered how much Hannah and Jennie loved chocolate covered graham crackers, "not the sweet kind, mind you."

We walked from the home place to the Methodist church which was locked up, but we were to get in later after a delightful visit with Muriel Gregory who had written to me ten years before. The Church had a new wing and was about to build a new sanctuary. We saw the choir loft where my Aunt Jennie sang alto and the old Sunday School rooms. There was a memorial plaque to George Cunningham in the vestibule.

Later we went to the Green Hill Cemetery to see the graves of John Michael and his wife Harriet, Hannah, Jennie, and Esther Lee. We did a rubbing of the main stone. There was a confederate marker on the grave, unceremoniously covered with what looked like grey radiator paint.

We then drove out into the country to a Presbyterian church named Stone's Chapel. There, to the rear of the cemetery, we found the stones of two of my great grandfather's brothers, Conrad and Michael, and their wives, but of them and how they came to live here we learned very little.

Yet there were many revelations on this trip and, as Mrs. Hart at one point said, "the record still stands".

This visit was at the height of the Civil Rights Movement. While in Green Hill Cemetery visiting the grave of my great grandfather marked with a Confederate emblem, I noticed nearby a prominently placed stone for Mammy Emily Early, "a faithful servant and friend to four generations." The stone captivated me and raised many questions about how slavery and the southern caste and class system might have played itself out in the life of my family, but it was too soon to ask and no one, at this point, was volunteering anything.

What was so striking about this visit, as well as the letters of 1962, was the warmth and intimacy of human recollection of events and remembrances of friends almost 60 years past:

- Mrs. Hart's recollection of the chocolate biscuits.
- Her placing flowers on the graves.

- E.G. Coiner, of department store fame, remembering that "the girls were delicate" (from the letters).
- Mrs. Hugh G. Owens, a friend, remembering my great grandmother as a "fine looking old time lady with lovely white hair".
- Hugh Owens remembering John Michael Pope as a tailor who was "very faithful to his church and attended regularly although very deaf." When asked why he attended worship when he couldn't hear, he replied that "it is just as important to be at my church as it is to be at my business."
- Mrs. Owens remembering that both Hannah and Jennie were fond of hot rolls and that she "had a pan that [she] filled and baked for them many times."

And so the curiosity, the warmth and emotion and the questions about these people and this place called Berryville grew deeper as the years passed.

Main Street Berryville as we discovered it for the first time in 1971.

The Duncan Memorial Methodist Church 1971

4

Through the Years

Berryville continued as legend in my life for the next 35 years. I told all of the stories that we knew to our children, Sarah and Ethan, and they always seemed interested but never attained the emotional attachment of my own childhood. They were growing up in a world that often seemed one hundred light years away from those early New Haven days.

We developed the strange habit of stopping in at Berryville whenever it was on the way to some other destination. These visits were, for the most part, without agenda. Each time, however, we met new people who shed light on the Pope family or the town history. I would always walk the length of Main Street conjuring up a sense of the past and the spirits of my ancestors, pay homage at the graves that I knew, drive by the family homestead, out to Stone's Chapel, and drop in at Coiner's Department Store that later became a gift shop before closing for good.

Without fail, I would stop for breakfast or lunch at Jane's Lunch, a family owned American diner on Main Street. Founded in 1942, the current owner, Mitzie Myers, has done a great job of maintaining the ambience of a mid 20th century Southern Main Street eatery. Indeed, locals continue to gather there most weekday mornings.

Remember the trunk photo of Mrs. Province McCormick, wife of the Indian Inspector? One day on a trip south with my younger brother, Robert, we were having breakfast at Jane's while a group of locals were gathered for coffee. We were looking over some Berryville family photos when a woman approached us, introduced herself as Henrietta Whiting and extended a warm welcome to town - a gesture that reminded me of the old New Haven tales about how people were friendlier *down south*. She called over to her husband, Richard, who came and sat with us in the booth and we showed him the photos including Mrs. Province McCormick. "That's my Grandmother!" he exclaimed "I have never seen a photo of her!" Later on that afternoon Mr. and Mrs. Whiting invited us to tea and took us on a whirlwind tour of the town, introducing us around to many people. While Richard, or "Bev" as he is called, knew that his grandfather had been the "Indian Inspector," we parted not knowing much more in the way of details.

It was later in this time frame that the internet emerged as well as web sites such as ancestry.com and television programs such as "Who Do You Think You Are?" More and more information became available, distant cousins were traced down and met, and answers to years of questions were found. We cruised Berryville with descendants of our ancestors' friends and made new friends of our own.

The confirmation of many of the truths of the old myths, the reasons for the emotions, and the true story of the Pope family as they lived the history of the town of Berryville, the Confederacy, and the nation itself, were coming together. The story was rich. The streets of Berryville still echoed with their footsteps and the serene countryside, largely unchanged, still beckoned with its tranquility and the lingering presence of those who celebrated life there so long ago.

I found Berryville not without some claim to national fame. It is known far and wide for equestrian events such as fox hunting. Well known Americans such as Harry F. Byrd, former Senator and Governor of Virginia, Drew Gilpin Faust, President of Harvard University and an antebellum and Civil War scholar, as well as Oliver North, had Berryville connections.

I discovered that while I was growing up in New Haven, Rennard (Rennie) Davis was growing up in Berryville. A leader during the anti Vietnam movement, he helped organize massive civil disobedience demonstrations including the protests at the 1968 Democratic National Convention and was indicted as one of the Chicago 7.

In 2011, Berryville gained more widespread national fame through an ad campaign promoting the Wendy's hamburger chain's Berry Almond Chicken Salad and Wild Berry Tea. The ad depicted a party on Main Street celebrating these concoctions. The town's name actually has nothing to do with berries and it was an almost comical bit of commercialism but it put Berryville on the national map.

At that point I decided it was time to write my family history, my small town sense of place history, my American history. "Carry Me Back to Old Virginia" had come full circle. This time, however, not in the form of emotional over indulgence, but in a story of wider interest that leads us back to German immigration, the antebellum south, Methodists and evangelicals of the Second Great Awakening, Confederate nationalism, the Civil War, American apartheid and the heady mix of life in small American southern towns during the 19th and 20th centuries. What follows is the story of what I learned.

CARRY ME BACK TO OLD VIRGINNY

Carry me back to Old Virginny
There's where the cotton and the corn and taters grow,
There's where the birds warble sweet in the springtime,
There's where this old darkey's heart am long'd to go.
There's where I labored so hard for old Massa,
Day after day in the field of yellow corn,
No place on earth do I love more sincerely
Than old Virginny, the state where I was born.

Chorus
Carry me back to old Virginny
There's where the cotton and the corn and taters grow,
There's where the birds warble sweet in the springtime,
There's where this old darkey's heart am long'd to go.

Carry Me Back to Old Virginny
There let me live 'til I wither and decay,
Long by the old Dismal Swamp have I wandered,
There's where this old darkey's life will pass away.

Massa and Missis have long gone before me,
Soon we will meet on that bright and golden shore,
There we'll be happy and free from all sorrow,
There's where we'll meet and we'll never part no more.

This song was adapted in 1878 by the black minstrel James Bland from the original which was frequently sung by Confederate soldiers during the Civil War. In 1916 a version by Alma Gluck was the first celebrity recording to sell one million copies. It was later a big hit for Ray Charles, Frankie Lane, and Jerry Lee Lewis. The civilian marching band of Virginia Tech continues to perform the song widely.

From 1940 until 1997 a reworded version was Virginia's state song. It was retired to emeritus status on the grounds that the lyrics were considered offensive to African Americans (despite the fact that it historically was written by a black man).

My childhood memory of my family's use of the song had nothing to do with race, but the ability of the catching emotional tune to strike golden chords of memory and love for a place. Ironically, the same memory and love is held by the former slave who sings it. The revered tune is very much in the tradition of Steven Foster's "My Old Kentucky Home" whose revised words are sung with the same affection on Kentucky Derby Day.

5

JOHANN MICHEL POPP

To begin the tale of what I discovered on my journey, I have to take you back to Germany in the early 19th Century. Between 1815 and the eve of the Civil War, two million German speaking Europeans migrated to the United States. As early as 1851, a group of German communities actually petitioned Congress to declare the United States a bilingual republic.

The initial impetus for this human tidal wave was the ruination left by the Napoleonic Wars and a host of other religious, economic, political, and social forces. From 1815 on, by the hundreds of thousands, villagers and city–dwellers from Germany sought a new future, and their overwhelming choice was America.

Migration, sweet though its hope, was a difficult step. Unsanitary sailing boats spread disease and human deprivation. It is estimated that a sixth of the passengers died aboard the ships and were buried on the high seas. Such conditions did not deter them, however, as they believed the end to be worth the risk. For some, even the prospect of two years of indentured service in order to repay the cost of transportation was considered cheap.

On October 12, 1841, one such immigrant, 60 year old Johann Michel Popp of Helmstadt, Germany, arrived at Baltimore, Maryland, on the ship *Louise*. His point of departure had been Bremen, Germany. The passenger and immigration lists state that his destination was Lancaster, Pennsylvania. Traveling on board the *Louise* with Johann Michel were his four children, Michel (later Michael) age 14, Conrad age 20, Babethe (later Barbara) age 11 and John Michel age 8.

Johann Michel Popp was born on May 13, 1781 at Helmstadt in the German state of Bavaria. Located in southeastern Germany, Bavaria was, historically, a fiefdom of the Holy Roman Empire and remained staunchly Catholic during the Protestant Reformation. The Popps, being no exception, were decidedly Roman Catholic and it is in church records that we are able to locate and trace them.

Johann Michel had outlived four wives and 11 children when he arrived in America with four of his surviving children by his fourth wife, Ursula Wander. He listed his occupation on the ship's log as "farmer," which helps us to understand what his situation was in Southern Germany.

6

Aus Deutschland

When the Napoleonic wars ended in 1815, wartime markets for certain products collapsed and competition from cheaper British products grew as they were once again allowed back into Europe. Masses of soldiers released from German armies went back to their farming areas and soon there was not enough viable farm land and work to go around. Prices started to rise but wages did not. There was a 50% rise in the prices of basic items like rye, potatoes and clothing. In addition, the blight that struck the potato crops of Ireland also hit southern Germany hard.

Michael Friedrich Radke, a German farmer, in a diary he started a few years after Johann Michel Popp left with his family for America, reflected on why he, too, was going to immigrate with his children to America. His words illuminate for us why Johann Popp possibly had done so as well.

"During my lifetime I had to fight through severe trials…and war's devastation…I worked day and night and walked in many places, spent many a sleepless night and the money I earned there was scarcely enough to feed my family…At the same time I saw thousands emigrate to….America….When thinking about it more closely, I realized that all of these emigrations were nothing more than the fault of the poverty that progressed with gigantic steps.

It was my desire to bring my children to a place where they could find work and bread….work hard and be frugal and …could prepare for a happy and calm future. In Germany the poor man is like a despised creature, or like a scarcely creeping worm, who must slither and creep along in the dust in order not to be stepped on to death. So it is that the poor man must adjust himself and bend himself to the rich who nevertheless scarcely notice him! The poor man slaves for the rich one, but what does he earn at days end? Only $7^{1/2}$ Groschen - which is 20 cents in American money and with that pay his rent and pay his royal taxes. If he does not pay punctually, all that he owns is taken away from him by officials of the law before whom he must appear in a bent position and with a bare head.

What will become of the poor children? How many of them have to beg for their daily bread in front of people's doors? Parents who are still able to send their children to school have to pay the school up until the children are 14 years of age, money for books clothing food and drinks. And after school is over what is one to do with the children? They have learned professions where they are treated like dogs to suffer hunger and thirst, and if they survive the miserable years of apprenticeship what do they have? They become journeymen and they go to beg bread in strange places before the doors of other people....The highest income per week 1 Thaler- 62 cents in American money. Or are the children to go into service and work for an entire year for nothing more than 6, 12, or 16 Thaler?" [1]

These are just a few reasons that Germans, many of whom had never before set foot out of their small villages, embarked on journeys that would change their lives and the life of their adopted country forever.

7

AUSWANDERING

Immigrating to America was more than simply a voyage. It was a whole set of adventures which could prove dangerous, even lethal. For most German immigrants, like Johann Michel Popp, Bremerhaven in northwestern Germany was the major point of departure.

The harbor in the city of Bremen proper had been silting up since the 16th century and, by the beginning of the 19th century, large ships could no longer reach the city docks but instead had to put in at smaller harbors along the Elbe north of Bremen. One of these, Bremerhaven, had been established as a port for the city of Bremen about four years before Johann Michel Popp and his family set sail.

Bremerhaven, the old harbor

The first leg of the Popps' journey would have been the trip to Bremen itself. Some poorer immigrants walked to the harbors. Michael Pope (formerly called Michel) in later years recalled climbing into a wagon to travel to Bremen. Many had never set foot outside their small villages and just taking this first step was in itself a life-changing experience. Once in Bremen, most would stay at an inn and take in the sites. Surely Johann Michel and his family would have gazed upon the statue of Roland that stands to this day in the market square. Created in 1404 to commemorate the death of Roland killed while attacking the rear-guard of Charlemagne's army, the statue is an internationally recognized symbol of liberty and freedom. It is perhaps ironic that the Popp family would soon be settling in Clarke County, Virginia, where 55% of the population was enslaved.

While trade between Bremen and America had already been established by the time the port of Bremerhaven opened, there was a significant trade imbalance due to the fact that Bremen had little to export with its underdeveloped hinterland and poor transportation network to get what goods there were to harbor. The business of transporting emigrants, therefore, was very important for the Bremen shipping community which had as its primary goal importing American goods to Germany. Ships from Bremen picked up tobacco and flour in Baltimore and tobacco, cotton and sugar in New Orleans. In the 1830s and 40s, Baltimore had particularly strong ties with Bremen with more immigrants arriving there at Henderson's Wharf in Fell's Point than in New York.

It is said that when ships such as the *Louise* departed, the emigrants stood in eerie silence on the decks watching their Fatherland slowly disappear. With differing degrees of sadness, joy, fear and optimism they faced several weeks at sea from Bremen to America barring any emergencies or accidents. Once they left land, they sailed into the North Sea and on to the English Channel, then out into the Ocean. Finally, many long weeks after the Bremen departure and half way around the world, America would be before their eyes.

There were few laws governing safety, feeding or cleanliness on board these ships and storms were frequent and often fatal. Ship fires were also common, as were other accidents and collisions. The emigrants, some with many children, were crammed into steerage, often sharing an uncomfortable wooden bunk with two or three other passengers for weeks.

If there were toilets, they were usually up on deck and hard to reach for the young, old and ill as well as for everyone else in stormy weather. The more usual facility in steerage, however, consisted of a few buckets with privacy screens. Cooking grates were set up on deck for steerage passengers who had to take turns using them in order to prepare a meal and were required to provide their own food. Diseases and illness spread quickly. The legislation governing slave ships from Africa was often more humane than the legislation governing these emigration ships. By law, the same ships which often carried in excess of 750 emigrants would only have been allowed to carry 500 slaves.

It was not uncommon for immigrant vessels to arrive with the entire ship full of ill, dying or dead passengers, or for the passengers to die while anchored in the harbor in quarantine. Indeed, the odors aboard these immigrant ships were so foul that people on land claimed they could smell them coming.

We can hope that the Popps fared better. In fact, Bremerhaven was one of the better ports from which to ship out. The Bremen senate at the time had begun to set up rules regarding the seaworthiness of the ships departing from her harbors, including minimum space requirements and that there be adequate provisions for three months at sea. They also required a doctor be on board for each voyage and mandated sanitary inspections.

Despite all the hardships, those like the Popps who survived the voyage were rewarded when they arrived in America with "its coast of thick forests, swarms of big fish, sea and water birds … geese and ducks … houses, windmills, beautiful green fields, blossoming fruit" and the promise of new life in a new world. [1]

8

A New Home in America

In the United States Census of 1850 we find the Popps living in Berryville, Clarke County, Virginia, in the area of Stone's Chapel and "Arabia," a decidedly isolated and rural area that, despite nearby modern sprawl, is somewhat unchanged today. The area was populated by many German and Scotch Irish immigrants. It is about one mile from the present day West Virginia line, ten miles from Charles Town, West Virginia, 16 miles from Harpers Ferry, West Virginia, and about 12 miles east of Winchester, Virginia.

As a worshipping community, Stone's Chapel was the first German church in Virginia. Lutherans, led by Thomas Hunsiker and Jacob Stone (Stein), formed a congregation in the early-to-mid 18th century that was served by itinerant pastors, since there were only about 16 ordained Lutheran pastors in the colonies.

Christian Streit became pastor here in 1785 preaching his first sermon in German at Stone's Chapel on August 7th. Streit, born in 1749 in New Jersey, had graduated from the Academy College in Philadelphia and studied with early Lutheran divines Henry Muhlenberg and Provost Wrangel. Ordained in 1770, he served with the 8th Virginia Regiment during the Revolutionary War. He came to Winchester in 1785, serving Winchester, Strasburg, Woodstock and Stone's Chapel. An extensive diary survives detailing his ministry.

In 1785 the German Lutherans in the region joined forces with the Presbyterians, who had been worshipping in the area since as far back as 1735, forming a partnership and meeting in a barn on the property deeded to them by Jacob and Barbara Stone. They used the barn and a wooden structure that they built until 1848 when they built the building that still exists today.

The Popps were Roman Catholics, of which there were few, if any, in this area. There is no indication that they participated in the life of this chapel, but it was a strong presence in the area and several family members rest in the churchyard.

Arabia is an area within this district comprising a narrow strip west through Brucetown and Clear Brook. The area of Stone's Chapel and eastward are considered the fringes of Arabia, where soil conditions are poor, rain is often lacking and only scrub pines and cedars grow.

How the Popps found their way to Berryville is unknown. The ship's log listed them with a destination of Lancaster and we do know that many Germans made their way to Berryville via Pennsylvania.

There was a practice in Germany, now referred to as "chain immigration," whereby people willing to emigrate were invited by family or friends to come to America where it was easier to earn a living. It is possible, therefore, that the Popps had friends already in Berryville and we know that there was communication back and forth as parish records in Helmstadt indicate that family members "died in America."

We also know that Johann Michel Popp was not the first member of the family to immigrate. He was preceded by his son, Jacob, in 1840. Jacob's mother was Johann Michel's first wife, Anna Maria Stumpf. According to Helmstadt parish records, Jacob died in the US in 1845. Where and how he lived here is unknown.

By the time of the census, the family had chosen to anglicize their name to Pope, not surprising as this is a prominent name in Virginia. Johann Michel was living with his daughter Babbethe, now Barbara, married to Adam Greenwalt who was also born in Germany.

Johann's son Michael is married to Elizabeth Swartz, and his other son Conrad is living nearby with his wife, Mary. Mary and Elizabeth Swartz were sisters with older roots in the area. There is some evidence that their mother was a Quaker. All the men, including Johann Popp who is now 73, are listed as agricultural laborers on nearby farms. The sons were beginning to create large families with a number of children already born to each. Many of their descendants continue to live in Berryville.

Johann's youngest son, John Michael, now 16, was indentured as a tailor. Indentured servitude was a system in which a parent legally gave over custody of a child to someone else in exchange for the promise that the child would be properly cared for and also taught a trade or skill to make a living as an adult. John Michael was being lovingly reared by Hannah and Manuel Showers in a boarding house (until recently the Battletown Inn) built in 1800 by the daughter of the town's founder. Berryville actually began here in the eighteenth century as a crossroads settlement known as Battletown. It is here in this slave owning household, exposed to hundreds of travelers and the news of the times, that young John Michael became immersed in the ways of his adopted homeland and laid the foundation for becoming a true spiritual patriot of Virginia. His life and the lives of his children were to parallel the history of Berryville into the first quarter of the twentieth century.

Nearby, in the area of Winchester known as Shawnee, the family was to be joined in 1852 by Kilian and his wife-to-be, Christina Bund. Born in 1823 at Helmstadt, Kilian was the grandson of Johann Popp and half nephew to Michael Jr., Conrad, Barbara and John Michael. His name attests to the family's Catholicism as St. Kilian, a missionary from Ireland, is credited with bringing Christianity to Bavaria. Kilian was a stone mason or brick layer. As a Catholic bachelor, he had been a member the Royal Bavarian 12th Infantry Regiment of King Otto of Greece. During the Civil War he was destined to end up in Yankee prison at Fort McHenry.

We turn now to look at a brief history of the area in which the Pope family found itself.

**The area around Stone's Chapel where the Popps settled
after 1850 is little changed in the present day.**

9

From Frederick to Clarke County in the Early Days

"We have discovered Paradise…"
Virginia Governor Spotswood 1716

Based on accounts beginning in 1600, the area in which the Popps settled was covered by thick forest. Native legend told of a valley with a beautiful river long referred to as Shenandoah, "Daughter of the Stars." For 10,000 years prior to the arrival of European explorers and traders, the indigenous people would seasonally trap and trade throughout the area.

The country also had vast prairie and afforded pasture for wild animals including game such as buffalo, elk, deer, panther, fox, beaver and wild fowl. This was especially true of the area that was to become the county of Clarke.

An English royal charter inherited by Thomas Lord Fairfax had granted over five million acres of land west of the Blue Ridge Mountains to include all land between the head waters of the Potomac and the Rappahannock rivers to the Chesapeake Bay. Fairfax's holdings were managed by Robert "King" Carter, the wealthiest and most influential man of his day. In 1730, a Fairfax land patent was issued to Carter's heirs.

As the population increased, the settlers sought to establish local government and in 1738 the Virginia House of Representatives created Frederick County encompassing the entire lower Shenandoah Valley. The first settlers came from Maryland, New Jersey and Pennsylvania and were Scotts-Irish, English Quakers, and Germans. Also, some of the gentry from along the James River settled in the upper end of the county.

Soon after arriving in Virginia, Lord Fairfax began to take steps to determine the status of his holdings and to sell and to rent out tracts of land. He met and was impressed by a young George Washington, then 16, and employed him to survey the sold and leased tracts of land. Washington's journal is full of reflections on the lower Shenandoah Valley which he later referred to as "the garden of America."

It is interesting to note, however, that Washington felt that Lord Fairfax was not living or behaving as a Baron should and that his chosen neighbors of rude Germans and unruly Scotch-Irish were "a parcel of barbarians, an uncouth set of people." [1]

By the 1750s a global rise in commodity prices created a huge demand for grain. Prominent Virginia Tidewater planters sought to profit from the original Fairfax grant and force marched their African slaves almost 200 miles to the west to clear and plant vast fields and build farms and mills in the limestone soils that were ideal for the cultivation of wheat.

These slaves and their ancestors had been kidnapped from western Africa and sold off slave ships on the James River to the wealthy plantation owners. After the Tidewater planters arrived, the area had more slaves within its land area than anywhere in Virginia and they played a significant role in the development of the region.

These Tidewater planters who lived in the eastern section of Frederick County were Virginians who functioned outside of what we today know as American democracy. Their ideal was an aristocratic republic in which superior individuals would rule the many. This concept of a social order was the first in America dating from 1607 at Jamestown. While these men had risked their lives in the American Revolution, they wanted personal liberty from the British king but not change in their social order. They were aristocrats who loved history but hated equality. They would have preferred Washington as king. The Civil War was to end their privileges and personal use of power and their social order bound by patterns of class subordination.

These were years of huge growth and change in the United States. Baltimore and Washington were growing at a fast pace. Everything that farmers raised, livestock or grain, could be sold if it could be gotten to market. Wagon trains and droves of cattle moved to the eastern cities. Prosperous stores were opened and efforts to provide education were undertaken.

The use of the Shenandoah increased with the opening of the Georgetown to Cumberland canal and, shortly afterwards, the building of the railroad to Harpers Ferry and westward. Ferries across the Shenandoah connected roads to the port of Alexandria. Flatboats were passing to Harpers Ferry and unloading onto canal or railway.

Beginning in about 1840, the state undertook internal improvements and a road was built from the Shenandoah River through Berryville to Winchester and on to Charles Town. By 1850 these roadways were finished, providing easy access to the entire area and beyond.

As wheat reigned supreme, the county's economy literally boomed, and slavery along with it, until over half the population of the area was enslaved, and the economy dependent on it.

As Frederick County developed, stark differences between the Tidewater settlers and those of the rest of Frederick County emerged, and in the early 1830s residents in eastern Frederick County petitioned Virginia to form their own county.

The reason for the split goes deeply into American, Virginian and local politics and history and has to do with states rights, slavery, interpretations of the constitutions of Virginia and the United States, economics, and the self sufficient farms and self reliant frontier democracy that tended to comprise western Frederick County.

Out of these controversies Clarke County was born in 1836. Named for Revolutionary War hero George Rogers Clark, elder brother of Second Lieutenant William Clark of the Corps of Discovery/Lewis and Clark Expedition, its 174 square miles made it one of the smallest counties in Virginia. Basically it appears that it was a social order in which the slave owning gentry held sway over all matters of public concern.

Clarke chose to locate its county seat at Berryville, a small town at the intersection of the Winchester Turnpike and the Charles Town Road. It consisted of about 30 homes, an apothecary, an academy, and two taverns. There, in 1842, they erected an English Georgian style courthouse designed by David Meade.

In earlier days this area had been given the informal name of Battletown due, some say, to the presence of a rowdy tavern where over indulgence by local yokels from adjoining plantations and town bullies led to violent fights that spilled out onto the street. Legend has it that Daniel Morgan (1736 - 1802), an aggressive leader of continental troops during the American Revolution who arrived in Clarke County with his family around 1750, joined in these battles.

The area had been granted by the crown in 1734 to Captain Isaac Pennington who, 20 years later, sold it to Colonel John Hite. Hite sold the tract in 1765 to his son-in-law, Major Charles Smith, who also named his estate Battletown to commemorate his participation in the Revolutionary War and built his clapboard homestead, Soldiers Rest, on the site of the former tavern. This house, now known as "The Nook," still stands on Main Street.

In 1797, Major Smith's son, John, sold 20 acres of his inheritance to Benjamin Berry and his daughter, Sarah Stribling, who divided it into lots for a town which was established as Berryville on January 15, 1798.

Sarah Stribling built her own home here in 1800 and turned it into a boarding house in 1805. It was bought by Charles Showers in 1811. It is here in 1850 at this house and this intersection that we find 16-year-old John Michael Pope.

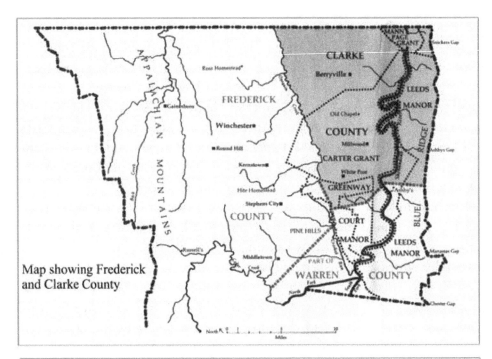

Map showing Frederick and Clarke County

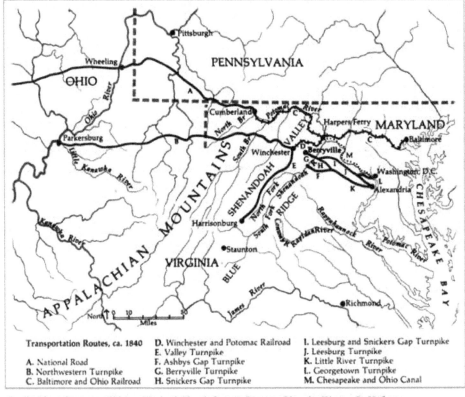

Transportation Routes, ca. 1840

A. National Road
B. Northwestern Turnpike
C. Baltimore and Ohio Railroad
D. Winchester and Potomac Railroad
E. Valley Turnpike
F. Ashbys Gap Turnpike
G. Berryville Turnpike
H. Snickers Gap Turnpike
I. Leesburg and Snickers Gap Turnpike
J. Leesburg Turnpike
K. Little River Turnpike
L. Georgetown Turnpike
M. Chesapeake and Ohio Canal

Credit: Maps Courtesy of Nancy Morbeck Haack from A Separate Place by Warren R. Hofstra

10

JOHN MICHAEL POPE AT BERRYVILLE

In 1850 John Michael Pope, who came to America in 1842 at eight years of age, is indentured as a tailor at the home of Emmanuel and Hannah Showers. As we have seen, this building was built by Sarah Stribling, daughter of Benjamin Berry, in 1800 and was turned into a boarding house in 1805.

Charles Showers bought the house in 1811, the year of his marriage, and the house remained in the Showers family until 1919.

The structure is located a block from the very intersection where Battletown was originally formed (Church and Main Streets). Near here stood the legendary rowdy tavern that gave the town its original name.

John Michael is being raised by the Showers, and we can easily surmise that it was a loving and encouraging relationship as in later years John Michael's first born daughter is given the name Hannah Showers Pope.

Unlike his father and older siblings who are living somewhat isolated lives out towards Arabia and Stone's Chapel, young John Michael finds himself at the crossroads of all the sociological and religious forces that are to shape the Civil War and indeed the course of American history.

Emmanuel Showers owns three slaves, 26 and 12 year old females, and a 65 year old male. Hardly a plantation, but an integral part of the household and of John's day-to-day living.

Within a short walk is the new Georgian Court House designed by David Meade. It was built by slaves who made up about 55% of the population of the new county. These slaves lived on self sufficient plantations to the west of the town and were carpenters, blacksmiths, stone masons and fence builders as well as domestic servants. They had no rights to the products of their labors. There was, in many instances, a strong sense of paternalism and mutual affection between slave and master.

While this romantic view may have been true, and many early historians often present it as the factual truth, most slave owners here and in the South didn't have any idea as to what many of their slaves really thought about their servitude. Many slaves believed that God would liberate them from white America. Laborers in the fields sang of themselves as a people born of a God who would liberate them from their bondage.

All was not totally harmonious in Clarke County and the fact that the new county philosophically and politically was built on the backs of these slaves is undeniable.

Undoubtedly because of the proximity of the Court House, the family must have rubbed shoulders with the slave owning gentry who dominated the rule of the new county. Indeed, Pope family records name many of their descendants as friends.

Commerce was in walking distance. Wagon making shops, cabinet makers, blacksmiths and tailors including Joseph Noble who lived in one of Berryville's oldest houses known as the House Upon the Rock built by Major Charles Smith in the mid 1700s. Noble, a Methodist, would host early meetings of that denomination here. On April 9, 1858, at the age of 24, John Michael would open his own tailor shop here.

Nearby was the old Academy founded in 1810, also a site of Methodist meetings, and within a stone's throw a number of other churches including the Presbyterian, Baptist, and Episcopal. It was the Methodist Church and the Evangelical Revival sweeping the Valley, and indeed the country, that was to have a profound influence on the life of young John Michael and his family.

The House on the Rock, c. 1754. Home of Joseph Noble. Early Methodist meetings were held here. John Michael Pope's tailor shop (April 9, 1858)[1.]

Early photo of the Showers House first occupied by Sarah Stribling in 1800 who turned it into a boarding house in 1805. Charles Showers bought the house in 1811 and it remained in his family until 1919. Here, in this slave owning household, John Michael Pope was apprenticed and lovingly raised. During the Civil War the house was vacated, occupied by soldiers and used for a time as a hospital. For a number of years it was operated as the Sign of the Motorcar Inn and, from 1954 until about 2013, as the Battletown Inn.

Photographs courtesy of Clarke County Historical Association

11

Evangelical Southern Methodism

"I can remember it was said by Mr. Matthew Jones who was a pillar in the Presbyterian church here, that if the Lord ever came to Berryville he would certainly visit at the home of John Michael Pope."

Esther S. Hart in a letter to Arthur Pope, August 19, 1962

In 1972 while visiting Esther S. Hart, granddaughter of Barbara Pope Greenwald, she narrated how the family of John Michael Pope was very religious. She even quipped "too religious."

This fits in nicely with the fact that many historical and other references to this branch of the Pope family are dominated by the themes of the Second Great Awakening and the Evangelical and Methodist revivals of the antebellum period. Many family members outside of the spectrum of Esther Hart's quip often thought of their religion as excessive. I remember my grandmother Minnie complaining in a slightly sarcastic manner that when she visited Berryville or when my great aunt Virginia visited New Haven it was politely requested that my grandmother hold forth with hymns on the piano all Sunday afternoon.

Nevertheless, religion, the Second Great Awakening and Methodism had a major impact on societal development in Berryville, Clarke County, the Shenandoah Valley and the nation itself.

Following the American Revolution, interest in religion was on the decline with well under ten percent of the population belonging to local congregations. Religion had been dealt a strong blow by Deists, most notably Thomas Paine. His pamphlet, *The Age of Reason*, questioned traditional supernaturalism and was as widely discussed as his earlier condemnation of rule by the British.

Change, however, was on the way in the form of a religious revival that swept the country from the mid 1790s onward.

In the opening frontier a great awakening took place due to the work of Presbyterians and itinerants from Baptist and Methodist churches. The revival spirit that transformed the beginning of the 19th century drew on the spirit of the American Revolution. Preachers called on individuals during this time to exert themselves for God. Finding traditional churches largely irrelevant, they organized voluntary societies to lead the nation to reform, winning the lost and expressing the country's democratic spirit.

"The broadest definition of evangelism includes everyone who believes that the second birth was essential for salvation – that none could enter heaven without a conscious emotional experience in which he accepted God's grace and dedicated his entire being to His glory." [1]

The obituary of Harriet Pope, John Michael's wife and my great grandmother, states it well. "Mrs. Pope was a lifelong member of the Methodist Church and had clearly defined views of religion. She was a faithful adherent of her church, yet free from all bigotry lived with her Lord. Faith in Jesus Christ her savior was not with her an occasional act but her spiritual attitude, the attitude of her life. Her life and her death [was] evidence of the reality of Christianity."

As much as 19th century evangelicals were shaped by doctrine they were also influenced by social factors and the location in which they lived. Curtis D. Johnson, in his book *Redeeming America,* organizes them into three major groups: Formalists, Anti-Formalists and African Americans.

Formalists were upper-middle-class Congregationalists, Presbyterians, low-church Episcopalians and English-speaking-reformed groups whose ultimate goal was to create a self-disciplined righteous republic whose law reflected the edict of God, sought an orderly faith that stressed consistent doctrine, decorum and worship and Biblical interpretation through a well-educated ministry. They were most powerful in the Northeast, the commercial and cultural center of the nation. They were, for the most part, anti slavery.

The Anti-Formalists comprised three fifths of Evangelical church membership, generally Baptists, Methodists and Disciples of Christ from the lower and middle classes, strong in the South and the West. This would include the John Michael Pope family. Theirs was an uncontrolled and unmanipulated emotional faith. They were deeply suspicious of elite attempts to Christianize society, to reform the nation, or in any other way improve America. For Anti-Formalists a Christian Republic would result in individual conversions by its citizens to a right relationship to God.

African Americans comprised one fifth of Evangelical church membership, were mostly Methodists and Baptists, largely enslaved and victims of severe prejudice. They combined African religious expression with Christianity and forged an evangelical belief system that sustained them during slavery and helped them form resistance to its ideology. They looked forward to the Jubilee when God would emancipate his people. This was undoubtedly the position of many of the enslaved in Clarke County. [2]

John Michael Pope was, first and foremost, a Methodist who fit into the Anti-Formalist category. He and his family bore allegiance to what had become in 1844 the Methodist

Episcopal Church South, a break from the North over the issue of slavery that lasted until 1939.

John Wesley, the founder of Methodism, was decidedly anti-slavery, "the execrable sum of all villanies" he called it, and when the denomination was founded in the United States in 1784 it officially opposed slavery. Wealthy Southerners, however, weakened the stance. In the early 1840s the Reverend James Osgood Andrew of Oxford, Georgia, a Methodist Bishop, acquired two slaves and was suspended. The controversy prompted Southern Methodists to break off and form a separate denomination.

Methodism had earlier been spurred on by English followers of John Wesley who was convinced that preachers should go where the gospel was most needed, exhorting his associates to go into every kitchen and shop and address all, aged and young alike, on the salvation of their souls. Methodism came to the United States in 1766 when Philip Embury, a Wesleyan convert from Ireland, began to preach in New York. Francis Asbury (1745 – 1816) arrived in 1771 and assumed leadership of the four Methodist workers already here.

While his colleagues favored a settled clergy located in populous areas, Asbury agreed with Wesley that preachers should go where the Gospel was most needed. Asbury's desire to spread the Gospel kept him on the move the rest of his life traveling nearly 300,000 miles on horseback. He crossed the Appalachians more than 60 times and it is said that more people in the American countryside knew Asbury than any other person of his generation.

His message can be summed up as emphasizing God's free grace, humanity's liberty to accept or reject that grace and the Christian's need to strive for perfection.

In the early 1800s Methodists had organized the Rockingham circuit of the Baltimore Conference as well as a Winchester circuit and these areas were visited often by Francis Asbury and other itinerant preachers. A Rev. Mr. Garvers was an early itinerant preacher at the home of Mr. A. M. Hardesty and Joseph Noble as well as at the old Academy at Berryville.

In 1838 a small group of Methodists formed a permanent congregation and purchased a building on a half acre of land that they used as a house of worship. This church was basically served by circuit riders until 1863. This was the group that influenced the young John Michael Pope and was later to form the Duncan Memorial Church (named for a Methodist Bishop) where the Pope family was to be active as the congregation mirrored life in Berryville.

From the author's personal collection

The Plantation Preacher

After the Civil War, Thomas Gold, Clarke County Historian, wrote that many of the African Americans "were sincere Christians and lived upright lives. Some who felt called to preach were so well taught that although unable to read they could repeat chapters of the Bible. The preachers were allowed to gather their families at night and on Sunday evenings and preach to them … encouraging them to take up the plan of salvation." [3] Gold's quotation, however, does not tell the whole story. In the black experience "singing is as close to worship as breathing is to life. [Their] songs of the soul and of the soil, have helped to bring a people through the torture chambers of the last three centuries." [4] While white slave owners loved the melodies and harmonies, they did not realize that their slaves were developing a theology of survival looking forward to liberation from an era of racism and oppression.

12

THE GATHERING STORM OF CIVIL WAR

Long years of American sectional debate had created an atmosphere of deepening hostility between North and South. During the stormy decade of the 1850s Americans faced each other with accelerated feelings of self-righteousness, hurt, pride and distrust. The corner of Church and Main Streets in Berryville was at the center of all of this.

Many argue that the Civil War was not about slavery, yet history proves that indeed not only the Civil War, but a major part of American history, has been about slavery. However, the argument that the average confederate waged war to preserve slavery is not sound. Most historians will point out that only six percent of southerners owned slaves and three percent of those owned the majority. Recruits themselves referred to the war as a "rich man's war and a poor man's fight."

John Michael's involvement in this great conflict was wrapped up in his religious beliefs, regional duty, state sovereignty, group solidarity and protection of home and family. He, like most of the rank and file of confederates, was probably detached from the horrors of slavery and was probably only familiar with the seeming love between slave and master and the religious philosophy that condoned it.

This allegiance to place was also where his brothers and their wives, Michael and Elizabeth Swartz and Conrad and Mary Swartz, found themselves although they were perhaps less aware of the religious and social forces that surrounded them on the plantations. For them local news came mostly from neighbors in face-to-face encounters and not so much from the heart of town. When war came it was about defense of their homes and family as they were laid low by Northern invasion. Neither Conrad nor Michael saw Confederate service.

With the advent of the fever of the Second Great Awakening, the evangelical formalists in the North advocated freedom for all people. "Year after year, Southern politicians and Southern leaders bitterly fought back. Here, of course, was a classic formula for eventual conflict. Where many in the North, notably the abolitionists, clamored for the eradication of slavery, Southerners clung ever more tightly to what they saw as the most treasured creed of republican liberty – property rights, including slaves." [1]

On Sunday, October 16, 1859, abolitionist John Brown, a descendant of Puritans and Revolutionary War soldiers, who saw the destruction of slavery as a fulfillment of American founding ideas, entered the town of Harpers Ferry, West Virginia (just a few miles north of Berryville) with 18 men. They took some of its prominent citizens hostage and captured the federal arsenal. His intention, as he later made clear, was to liberate the slaves in the surrounding territory and form them into an army which would then liberate all slaves throughout the South. On October 18th, United States Marines under the Command of Robert E. Lee, accompanied by his student at West Point, Lt. James "Jeb" Stuart, surrounded and killed or captured the insurgents. The long term effect on both Northern and Southern emotions far exceeded the wildest dreams of these insurgents. Accounts of the raid and the subsequent trial and execution of John Brown attracted national attention and the event became a symbol of both sides in the Civil War.

Treadwell Smith of Berryville noted in his diary on November 21, 1859, "Berryville under Martial Law. Sentries posted during the night at all corners of the different regular quartered military force in barracks." [2]

Enraged Southerners in Clarke County branded the raid an act of treason and terror. Several weeks after the affair, Charles White, minister of the Presbyterian Church at Berryville, Stone's Chapel and Harpers Ferry wrote a letter to his brother-in-law John Felt of Salem, Massachusetts. On Sunday evening October 16 he had preached his regular weekly sermon and was awakened the following morning to the disturbance in Harpers Ferry. He became an eyewitness and minor participant of all the events and in his letter drew maps and included a detailed eyewitness account. Of particular interest is his viewpoint of John Brown and the affair, all of which undoubtedly mirrors the thinking of people at Church and Main as well as in the Stone's Chapel area and throughout Clarke County.

In his letter, White wrote "I was at first inclined to think Brown a brave man – of some remnant of a generous nature – but the more I see and hear of his devilish designs, the more thoro' becomes my contempt and horror of him – and all his abettors & sympathizers, including Cheever, Beecher & Co. During the affair the negroes about H F were terribly alarmed and clung as closely as they could to master and mistress. One negro hid under a water wheel in the armory canal and didn't come out till Tuesday – and then was afraid Brown might catch him. One slave has since died of fright – whom Brown had prisoner. Some one or two slaves whom B had taken and given pilees (sic) in the engine house – on that fearful night, true to their natures dropped the pikes and went to sleep. Not one slave that we can discover was willingly with them – unless it be the one drowned. This shows well for the slaves I think. Those who were taken – escaped to their homes as soon as they got a chance. And not one woman was taken or freed – which is rather singular, when they had so good an opportunity – and loved them so. There is of course a great deal of excitement – and to add to it several stock yards – barns etc. have been burnt in the last week in our county – and several masters have been beaten or attacked by their servants.

But I believe the majority of servants have no evil intentions – or desire any movement. They know & say they are better off where they are & as they are. We have patrols out every night. Ch[arle]stown is guarded every night at every point. I do not think you need be uneasy about us. Have you seen Wendell Phillips speech in H. Ward Beechers church? It is the most atrocious – treasonable & murderous piece of villa[i]ny I have ever read. I suppose Beecher is as bad. I do not know that the Devil would display such malignity. There are a great many incidents etc I might mention – but it would perhaps be tedious. If you think of anything in regard to this you would like to ask – I shall be glad to answer. I wish I could see you all. You had better come down & take a look at the scene of action. These men must doubtless be hung." [3]

Almost 25 years later, White is still reflecting presumably on the sentiments of his communities including Harpers Ferry, Berryville and Stone's Chapel. He says, "I can hardly think anybody that saw and heard on the occasion of Brown's advent at Harpers Ferry – could think him conscientious even except with the understanding that it was a conscience deeply, darkly perverted by his demonish purposes and desires. It fell to my lot as Pastor at Harpers Ferry at that time, with true and kind intent, and to seek to minister to his spiritual wants, to go in to see John Brown, when captured and wounded and it was thought he would probably die. I was witness of the whole scene, fight, capture etc – and was familiar with the whole matter, having been in prison bounds by his two bands of ruffians. Some of my people were killed by him. I have no hesitancy in saying that after my personal interview with him then – and the many years of reflection since, my opinion is now what it was then – that there was no religious motive or even any truly philanthropic motive moving him to his dastardly, cowardly deed of shooting & killing innocent men, and forcing, as I personally know he did, negroes to carry two edged pikes for the slaughter of their own Masters. I have never been able to see but that he was an inexcusable and unmitigated murderer." [4]

On December 2nd, 1859, Treadwell Smith notes in his diary that "John Brown was hung today at Charlestown (sic) for insurrection and murder." Northern abolitionist Wendell Phillips spoke at John Brown's funeral in the Adirondacks in New York saying "History will date Virginia emancipated from Harpers Ferry. True the slave is still there. So when the tempest uproots a pine on your hills, it looks green for months – a year or two still it is timber and not a tree. John Brown has loosened the roots of the slave system; it only breathes. It does not live hereafter."

His words were prophetic for by 1861 John Michael Pope was caught up in the Confederacy in a patriotic fervor greater than the American Revolution itself. This new national spirit I believe is what was still echoing back to New Haven through family legend when I was growing up.

THE GATHERING STORM OF CIVIL WAR | 39

Harpers Ferry, 1859.
Image Credit: Historic Photo Collection, Harpers Ferry NHP.

Rev. Charles White, Minister of
Berryville Presbyterian Church and Stone's Chapel,
was present at Harpers Ferry the day of the raid and
wrote an eyewitness account of his reflections.

The last moments of John Brown.
By Thomas Hovenden. Sentimental portrait.

13

WAR

"Every patriot must keep his armor girded so long as the dastard foe invades the sacred soil of the South and desecrates the holy temple of liberty"

> William C. Carson, Virginia cavalryman

"The Confederate national identity in 1861 was actually far stronger than any collective American national identity alive at the time of the Constitution."

> John Murrin

As we have seen, John Brown's rash actions proved a foretaste of a greater action to come and Virginians began to arm themselves against what they perceived to be the onslaught of Northern aggression. A number of militia regiments were formed in Berryville, including a company that called themselves the Clarke Guards, whose immediate task was to guard the prison in Charles Town. It disbanded after Brown's execution. Shortly thereafter, a company was formed that called themselves the Clarke Rifles. They spent the fall and winter of 1860-61 drilling. During this period several Southern states seceded from the Union forming the Confederate States of America.

I have referred in previous chapters to some of the economic and political forces that shaped the Confederacy. It saw itself as having every aspect of its way of life being crushed by Northern political, banking and industrial powers. The 23 states that, in the end, remained in the Union had a combined population of 22 million. There were 100,000 factories employing 1.1 million workers. The Union possessed more than 20,000 miles of railroad and Union banks held 81% of the nation's bank deposits and 56 million dollars in gold.

The 11 Confederate states held a population of nine million including four million slaves. There were only 20,000 factories employing 100,000 workers and 9,000 miles of railroad track. The Union and the Confederacy were hugely divided by politics, economy and culture. All of these differences were generated by the institution of slavery.

The Union was racing ahead in banking, booming factories, maritime enterprise and a mushrooming population of Irish, German and other immigrants. The Southern states, like Virginia and Clarke County in particular, with their much weaker economic base, were, in a sense, standing still, stuck in an agricultural slave-based economy. They felt their liberty and way of life was being overpowered by the North. Emotions were high.

Many of the politicians of the Confederacy, made up of the slave owning class with the most to lose from emancipation, also threw into the mix a race-baiting hysteria including the idea that blacks would take control "and the certain sexual ravishing of Southern womanhood if slaves were allowed to go free…" [1]

The potent mix of economic fear and racially tinged emotions coalesced over the question of slavery. Even those in the Confederacy who held no slaves thought the powers of the North had no right to tell them how to live their lives. [2] Thus, with their political power diminishing in Congress and the overwhelming power of the free states growing, the Southern states had turned to what they perceived to be their most powerful weapon – Secession!

On April 12, 1861 Confederate batteries opened fire on the Federal Garrison of Fort Sumter, South Carolina. The Federal government vowed to use force to put down the rebellion. At this point, Virginia announced that it, too, would secede. Church bells rang. Cheering crowds in Winchester and throughout the Shenandoah Valley massed in the streets releasing tensions that had been building for years.

Shortly after secession Virginia Governor Letcher sent a telegram ordering local militia to seize the Federal Arsenal at Harpers Ferry and he issued a call for recruits to repel the invasion and protect the citizens of the state.

On the morning of the 17th of April 1861, the Clarke Rifles were ordered to report in uniform and with arms at Berryville by noon. There were hasty goodbyes and many tears shed by anxious mothers and wives over departing sons and husbands. But among the men, especially the young and naive, all was joy and hilarity. They had no idea of the terrible events which were soon to follow or of the long years of toil and danger that lay ahead. "We would soon settle matters and be at home again." [3]

In less than ten days the Clarke Rifles had joined up with enough other small units to officially form a brigade on April 27, 1861 (First Brigade Virginia Volunteers). Robert E. Lee, who became commander of Virginia's troops, appointed Colonel Thomas Jonathan Jackson as its commander.

By June of 1861, Treadwell Smith began taking note of the Confederate army camping near Berryville and records several visits to view them. In July, he reports 25-30,000 Federal troops encamped at Charles Town. Word came back to Berryville on July 21, 1861 that Thomas Jackson had been victorious at the First Battle of Bull Run (or Manassas). A wave of euphoria swept Berryville and the South. Jackson, who at this point had been christened "Stonewall," said to his men "you have gained a proud position in the history of this our second war of independence …" Little did Southerners know, however, that the Union now realized it was in for a major war and was beginning to amass an army of enormous strength.

At 1 o'clock in the afternoon of March 10, 1862, Federal troops took possession of Berryville. On March 11, 1862, 30 year old John Michael Pope who, at this point, had been a member of the 122nd Virginia Militia Regiment Company B, enlisted as a private in the Second Regiment Virginia Infantry that later became known as the Stonewall Brigade. This was shortly before conscription went into effect making him eligible for enlistment bonuses, choice of units and the comparative pride of entering service of one's free will.

John Michael stepped up to defend the Confederate States of America and joined those already fighting to preserve their political, social and economic ways. They wanted to maintain what had been and to be left alone with the status quo. The average Southerner, like John Michael, was not fighting to maintain slavery. Most of the Southern soldiers were farmers and laborers who took up arms to defend the home land.

With regard to slavery, they did feel that Northerners were hypocrites – vilifying Southerners for enslaving blacks while they kept millions of white factory workers in conditions far worse than slavery and, as we have seen, crowned the likes of John Brown with martyrdom when his avowed purpose was the wholesale murder of Southern men and women.

This is all a pretty heady mix of ideas but, after many years, I have concluded that these ideas were embraced by John Michael Pope and, furthermore, that his embrace of religion - especially Southern Methodism – added even more fire to the flames of his commitment and provided him with coping mechanisms during the war.

This postcard published by the Confederate Museum after an original painting by W. L. Sheppard depicts John Michael Pope's most likely appearance as a Confederate infantryman.

THE BONNIE BLUE FLAG

We are a band of brothers and native to the soil
Fighting for our Liberty, with pleasure, blood and toil
And when our rights were threatened, the cry rose near and far
Hurrah for the Bonnie Blue Flag that bears a single star!

Chorus:

Hurrah! Hurrah!
For Southern rights, hurrah!
Hurrah for the Bonnie Blue Flag that bears a single star!

As long as the Union was faithful to her trust
Like friends and like brethren, kind were we, and just
But now, when Northern treachery attempts our rights to mar
We hoist on high the Bonnie Blue Flag that bears a single star.

The Bonnie Blue Flag, also known as *We are a Band of Brothers*, is an 1861 marching song that refers to the unofficial first flag of the Confederacy. The flag was used by the State of Mississippi following the first week of secession. The song, second only to *Dixie* in the South, was written by Ulster-Scots entertainer Harry McCarthy. It was sung with great gusto by thousands of young Southern troops who had enlisted for 90 days eager to kill 20 Yankees before they finished the job and won the war.

14

ENLISTMENT

"During the Civil War, the Stonewall Brigade well earned its reputation as one of the elite units in American military history. In fact historians have since compared it to famous formations around the world such as Caesar's Tenth Legion, Napoleon's Old Guard or Alexander's Companion Cavalry …" [1]

In March of 1862, John Michael Pope begins his service as a private in the Second Virginia Infantry. This unit was mostly composed of volunteers from Jefferson, Clarke, Frederick and Berkely Counties of the lower Shenandoah Valley. The Second Regiment was a company within the full brigade formed on April 27, 1861. Three months later this brigade had earned its name, the Stonewall Brigade, in which 6,000 men were to serve throughout the war. Only 210 were to remain at the surrender at Appomatox four years later. Under the leadership of Jackson, the Brigade had distinguished itself in July of 1861 at the First Battle of Bull Run, or First Manassas. This victory for the Confederacy had caused a wave of euphoria to sweep the South.

At the time of John Michael's enrollment, Jackson's force was in winter quarters near Virginia. His first engagement with the regiment was to be the Battle of Kernstown in March of 1862, which proved to be Stonewall Jackson's only defeat. Kernstown was followed by the battles of Front Royal and First Winchester in May of 1862.

During this time, John Michael undoubtedly experienced not only the glory of war but its far greater horrors as well. We glean from the writings of fellow soldiers, both Northern and Southern, what conditions might have been like: foul weather, filth, lack of privacy, stern discipline and near starvation. These soon diminished the cheers of the crowds at Winchester seeing them off to war. Death and disease were everywhere.

And then there was the Baptism of Fire when one rushes into battle for the first time well described by a first timer: "With your first shot you become a new man, personal safety is your least concern, fear has no existence in your bosom. Hesitation gives way to an uncontrollable desire to rush into the thickest of the fight. The dead and dying around you, if they receive passive thought, only serve to stimulate you to revenge. You become cool and deliberate and watch the effect of bullets, the showers of bursting shells, the passage of cannon balls as they rake their murdering channels through your ranks … with a reeling so callous … that your soul seems dead to every sympathizing and selfish thought." [2]

In the midst of all this, men of an evangelical Christian faith like John Michael undoubtedly agreed with Louisiana Sergeant Edwin Fay who did not believe a bullet can go through a prayer "because faith was a much better shield than … steel armor." It was during this time period that the seeds of John Michael's affection for the two giants of the Confederacy, Lee and Jackson, depicted in those images found in the trunk in our New Haven attic, began to be sown.

15

ROBERT E. LEE

"He loved us like a father and led us like a king ... we trusted him as Providence and obeyed him like a god ..."

Confederate Veteran [1]

Amongst the most emotional of the remembrances and stories that came up to New Haven concern General Robert E. Lee who took control of the force he named the Army of Northern Virginia in June of 1862. These stories related that there had been encounters and conversations between John Michael Pope and Robert E. Lee. A story passed down was that my great grandfather promised Lee that any offspring he had would carry his name. Whether this conversation was imagined or not, it is true that the promise was kept. Given the accounts of Lee's personal encounters with his men from all walks of life, we can see the possibility of the legend's truthfulness.

The son of Revolutionary War officer Light Horse Harry Lee and top graduate of the United States Military Academy, Lee distinguished himself for 32 years in the United States Army, most notably during the Mexican American War and as Superintendant of the United States Military Academy. He was known as an exceptional officer and contact combat engineer. Offered command of a Union army by Abraham Lincoln and despite his personal desire for the country to remain intact, he chose to follow his home state into secession.

He originally served as Senior Military Advisor to the President of the Confederacy, Jefferson Davis. By the end of the war he had assumed supreme command of the remaining Southern armies.

Married to his deeply religious third cousin, Mary Anna Randolph Custis Lee who was born at "Annefield" in Clarke County (while her mother was traveling), Lee was a devout Episcopalian (although he did not join the church until the age of 42). He fully personified the great marriage of the Confederacy with religion explained in a Methodist tract that was designed to enable the South, "[l]ike a city set upon a hill [to] fulfill her God given mission to exalt in civilization and Christianity the nations of the earth." [2] This carried over to his views of slavery.

In a letter to Mary he states: "In this enlightened age there are few I believe, but what will acknowledge that slavery as an institution is a moral and political evil in any country. It is useless to expatriate on its disadvantages. I think it however a greater evil to white man than to the black race and while my feelings are strongly enlisted in behalf of the latter, my sympathies are strong for the former. The blacks are better off here than in Africa, morally, socially and physically. The painful discipline they are now undergoing is necessary for their instruction as a race, and I hope will prepare and lead them to better things. How long this subjugation may be necessary is known and ordered by a wise and merciful providence."

Thus Lee was to be found agreeing with most religious people of his class in Virginia who believed that slavery existed because God willed it and that it would end when God so willed. Lee, however, was never exposed to slavery nor spent any considerable time south of Virginia and was quite unfamiliar with the excesses of the institution further south. [3]

As I studied the life of Robert E. Lee, the meaning of all the family emotion became very clear. There are few men in the history of the world who have dominated a nation and left an imprint on its people in the way Robert E. Lee influenced the Confederacy. Lee, and the men like John Michael Pope who followed him, believed that ultimately their righteousness would prevail.

Robert E. Lee
Image hung on parlor wall, J.M. Pope homestead.

16

STONEWALL JACKSON

Stonewall Jackson was just the right personality for John Michael to idolize. Thomas Jonathan "Stonewall" Jackson was one of the great commanders in military history. Eccentric, ascetic, demanding and fearless he was one of those rare individuals who, in conflict, could stamp his own personality on the outcome of events, achieving victory for his cause against daunting odds.

Jackson was born in the back country of Virginia in 1824. Orphaned at age seven, Jackson and his sister, Laura, were sent to live with his uncle, Cummins Jackson, who owned a grist mill in Jackson's Mill near present day western West Virginia. Formal education was not easily obtained and much of his education was self taught before he became a school teacher. He once made a deal with one of his uncle's slaves to provide him with pine knots (which he burned to provide illumination to read borrowed books by night) in exchange for reading lessons. Although forbidden by law, he did teach the slave to write as promised and, once literate, the young slave fled to Canada on the underground railroad.

Jackson entered West Point in 1842 and, although he had served as a school master, his education was quite inadequate. However, while he almost failed his first year, he managed to finish 17th of 59 in his class. Jackson began his U.S. Army career in the Mexican American War (1846 – 1848) and earned the rank of major. In the Spring of 1851, Jackson had accepted a newly created teaching position at Virginia Military Institute in Lexington where parts of his curriculum are still taught. "Discipline, mobility, assessing the enemy's strength and intentions while attempting to conceal your arms, and the efficiency of artillery combined with an infantry assault." [1]

Jackson was not popular at the Institute, however. Students mocked his stern religious nature and his eccentric traits. His many biographers note his obedience to duty, scrupulous honesty, generosity and kindness, doggedness and oddities of posture and diet to relieve his obscure ailments (he had a belief in the therapeutic power of lemons). He was also extremely taciturn and capable of staring at a campfire for hours without saying a word. Little known to the white inhabitants, Jackson was revered by the African Americans in Lexington. In 1855 he organized a Sunday school for Blacks at the Presbyterian Church.

Stonewall Jackson was a perfect hero for young John Michael Pope to idolize in matters of religion, for Jackson was devout. A Deacon in the Presbyterian Church, he was known as a "Blue Light," a term applied to a military man whose evangelical zeal burned with the intensity of the blue light used for illumination at night. A biographer, Robert Lewis Dabney, suggested that it was the fear of God which made him so fearless of all else. Jackson himself said "my religious belief teaches me to be as safe in battle as in bed."

Another biographer, James S. Robertson, Jr., says of Jackson that he was a Christian soldier in every sense who thought of war as a religious crusade and viewed himself as an Old Testament warrior like David or Joshua who went into battle to slay the Philistines.

STONEWALL JACKSON'S WAY

(Found on the body of a Sergeant of the old Stonewall Brigade,
Winchester, Virginia)

Come, stack arms, men; pile on the rails,
Stir up the camp-fire bright;
No matter if the canteen fails,
We'll make a roaring night.
Here Shenandoah brawls along,
There burly Blue Ridge echoes strong,
To swell the brigade's rousing song,
Of "Stonewall Jackson's way."

We see him now – the old slouch hat
Cocked o'er his eye askew –
The shrewd, dry smile – the speech so pat –
So calm, so blunt, so true.
The "Blue Light Elder" knows 'em well –
Says he, "That's Banks; he's fond of shell –
Lord save his soul! we'll give him" – well
That's "Stonewall Jackson's way."

Silence! ground arms! kneel all! caps off!
Old Blue Light's going to pray;
Strangle the fool that dares to scoff;
Attention! it's his way.
Appealing from his native sod,
In forma pauperis to God –
"Lay bare thine arm; stretch forth thy rod;
Amen!" That's "Stonewall's way."

He's in the saddle now! Fall in!
Steady, the whole brigade!
Hill's at the ford, cut off! we'll win
His way out, ball and blade.
What matter if our shoes are worn!
What matter if our feet are torn!
"Quickstep – we're with him before dawn!"
That's "Stonewall Jackson's way."

Ah, maiden! Wait and watch and yearn
For news of Stonewall's band;
Ah, widow! read with eyes that burn
That ring upon thy hand;
Ah, wife! sew on, pray on, hope on,
Thy life shall not be all forlorn –
The foe had better ne'er been born,
Than get in "Stonewall's way."

Stonewall Jackson
Image hung on parlor wall, J.M.Pope homestead.

17

DESERTION AND ON TO FREDERICKSBURG

John Michael Pope's first taste of war came at the Battle of Kernstown on March 23, 1862. This was followed by what was called the Valley Campaign that included the battles of Front Royal and First Winchester that continued the Brigade's reputation as a primary instrument of strategic victory for the Confederacy.

On May 30th, just two months later, John Michael Pope is AWOL! He does not return to service until September 12th, three and a half months later.

I must admit that, when I first discovered his absence, I was filled with some anxiety. Research revealed, however, that the Stonewall Brigade had much higher desertion rates than other Confederate formations. This was due to the fact that most of its men were drawn exclusively from the Shenandoah Valley, a major avenue of operation for the Confederacy, affording the men easy access to their homes, families and neighbors.

Desertion was a significant problem within the Confederacy. However, while it was a major offense subject to court martial and all sorts of punishments such as being shot to death, whipped, head shaved, being drummed out of service, riding wooden horses and wearing barrel shirts, many men of the Brigade quietly slipped away to tend to business at home and, for the most part, officers looked the other way. Indeed, during this period (the Maryland Campaign) thousands of men deserted their colors. They were tired of fighting and marching and "some had a philosophical objection to invading the North since they had signed up in the defense of the South." [1]

What John Michael did during this time period is unknown. Nevertheless, he does return on September 13th and the record thereafter shows no signs of cowardice or fear or lagging allegiance to the cause. By the time of John Michael's return, many others had done so as well thereby swelling the ranks of the Brigade by five fold. And, best of all, despite the carnage, the Confederacy was on the way to victory.

At the Battle of Antietam, or Sharpsburg, on September 17th there were 23,000 casualties with hundreds later dying of their wounds. The Stonewall Brigade lost a third of its men.

On the first day of December, the Stonewall Brigade marched on to Fredericksburg where, in a decisive victory described to Abraham Lincoln as "butchery," the Union army suffered over 12,000 casualties to the Confederate 5,000. After the battle, the Stonewall Brigade went into Winter quarters a short distance west of Fredericksburg. The Winter was primarily marked by a wave of religious revivalism that swept the Confederacy.

After the battle of Fredericksburg in December 1862, the Stonewall Brigade went into Winter Quarters.

(Photograph: Library of Congress, Washington D.C.)

18

REVIVAL!

"Here [Winter Quarters] we had for the Brigade a large log house for preaching and during the winter a meeting of weeks during which many were converted … [I] had some very earnest and devoted Christians, among the best was JM Pope a good Christian and brave soldier. The influence of such men was far-reaching and inspiring to all who met them."

Thomas Gold [1]

Despite the fact that evangelical sects prevailed in the South and Confederate soldiers were mustered into service with hymns and prayers and gift Bibles to carry on their persons, religion did not thrive in the Confederate camps the first two years of the conflict. The harshness of army life quickly set in. A soldier's life was one of marching, drilling and fatigue. These mostly single 18 year olds accustomed to a life of independence were quickly feeling the lash of the officer's tongue and the sergeant's whip, a punishment that, prior to the war, was known only for slaves. Furthermore, thousands of men were dying of disease, not combat. Life in camp was depressing. Adventure was to be found in whiskey, cards, dice, and prostitutes.

Many seemed to be bored also with chaplains and religious services and wanted to spend their Sunday mornings cleaning up, putting their quarters in order, preparing their arms for inspection and writing home. But the evangelical churches at home were at work. "In fact, the southern evangelists were perhaps the most efficient and organized entity in the confederacy." [2] They provided the army with hundreds of thousands of pages of religious tracts and hundreds of preachers. A revival broke out that was to spread throughout the army of northern Virginia and beyond.

The revivals came at a time when Confederate morale had suffered defeats at Sharpsburg, Maryland and Perryville, Kentucky. Interlocked together in the revival were an acute awareness of sin, daily prayer meetings and church services, fervid exhortations by chaplains, visiting missionaries, soldiers and laymen, public confessions of wrong doing, baptisms at nearby streams, lines of men seeking conversion and even greater numbers reaffirming their faith. A Confederate described the revival as one great Methodist camp meeting "... they build log fires, sing, pray and preach, and when they ask for the mourners they come in hundreds some falling to the ground crying for mercy." [3]

It is important to realize that at the time the revivals began civilians and soldiers in the South were beginning to question the Confederacy's invincibility. The feelings were developing "that God would not permit the South to triumph unless and until her people humbled themselves, did genuine penance and committed themselves to the keeping of Providence." [4] This sentiment reached its peak immediately after Gettysburg and Vicksburg.

Even more importantly, however, was the prospect of death confronting the soldiers. Regiments such as the Stonewall Brigade were dwindling in numbers. Chances of a soldier surviving the battles yet to come were slim. Thousands (150,000 by some estimates) were answering the call to escape damnation and gain religious assurance of eternal peace.

Jefferson Davis, President of the Confederacy, Robert E. Lee and a great majority of southern military leaders joined Stonewall Jackson in support of the revivals out of their own religious persuasions but certainly also saw their value in regards to the soldiers' improved discipline, morale and conduct in battle. In contrast, the North saw no such large scale revival. It should be clearly understood, however, that the majority of Confederates made no profession of faith and had no church affiliation.

"Southern evangelicalism reflected the charismatic and independent character of the Appalachian farmers. Southern yeomen declared their independence from the staid faith of the plantation gentry ... who dominated politics and business." [5]

These revivals for men like John Michael Pope and others who experienced them did have a profound influence. "The Confederate soldiers dealt with the atrocities of a modern war fought with Napoleonic tactics. Friends ... were torn to bits right next to each other. Soldiers faced down cannon, rifled muskets, and bayonets across open field charges. Men could be killed by gunfire or disease. In an era before 'combat fatigue' and 'traumatic stress disorder' 19th century men turned to the best coping mechanism at hand, their faith." [6]

ON JORDAN'S STORMY BANKS

On Jordan's stormy banks I stand,
and cast a wishful eye
to Canaan's fair and happy land,
where my possessions lie.

Refrain:
I am bound for the promised land,
I am bound for the promised land;
Oh, who will come and go with me?
I am bound for the promised land.

O'er all those wide extended plains
shines one eternal day;
there God the Son forever reigns,
and scatters night away.
(Refrain)

No chilling winds or poisonous breath
can reach that healthful shore;
sickness and sorrow, pain and death,
are felt and feared no more.
(Refrain)

When I shall reach that happy place,
I'll be forever blest,
For I shall see my Father's face,
and in his bosom rest.
(Refrain)

Like Julia Ward Howe's *Battle Hymn of the Republic*, such favorites as 18th century hymn writer Samuel Stennett's *On Jordan's Stormy Banks I Stand* bolstered southern evangelicals as they faced the challenges of war.

19

CHANCELLORSVILLE

Late in April, 1863, Union General Joseph Hooker, with an army of 130,000 men, was ready to strike against Lee's 60,000 troops. On April 30th, Hooker reached the town of Chancellorsville making his headquarters at Chancellor House, an old plantation home surrounded by slave shanties.

Lee, after conferring with Stonewall Jackson who, at this point commanded 26,000 men, sent Jackson 12 miles past the Union front and around to its weakest spot while making a diversionary show of force against the center of Hooker's lines.

Hooker did notice Jackson but thought he was in retreat, that is until Jackson attacked at 5:15 pm, May 2nd, while the Union soldiers were lounging in camp, with their rifles stacked, playing cards. John Casler, a comrade of John Michael in the Second Brigade wrote:

"We ran through the enemy's camps ... Tents were standing and camp-kettles were on fire, full of meat. I saw a big Newfoundland dog lying in one tent as if nothing had happened. We had a nice chance to plunder their camps and search the dead ... which some did ... despite the need to keep up with the artillery." [1]

Jackson's rampaging troops swept nearly all the way to Hooker's headquarters. Perhaps one of the most horrifying events of the Civil War occurred when the brush in the thick tangle of woods caught fire trapping large numbers of wounded from both sides. One Union soldier wrote:

"I began to pull away from the burning brushwood and got some of them out. Them pines was full of pitch and rosin and made the fire as hot as a furnace ... The underbrush crackled and roared and the poor devils howled and shrieked when the fire got at them. The last I saw of [one] fellow was his face. His eyes were big and blue, and his hair like raw silk surrounded by a wreath of fire. I heard him scream 'O Mother! O God, God!' It left me trembling ... My [own] hands were so blistered and burned I could not open or shut them." [2]

Likewise, John Casler wrote on burial details. "We could see where they had tried to keep the fire from them by scratching the leaves as far away as they could reach. But it availed not, they were burned to a crisp. It was the most sickening sight I saw during the war and I wondered whether the American people were civilized or not, to butcher one another in that manner and I came to the conclusion that we were barbarians North and South alike." 3

Jackson's intent had been not only to push Hooker's flank but to insert his corps between the Union army and the US Ford on the river thus cutting them off from retreat. Trying to maneuver for such an advantage he rode to the front but was turned back by Union forces. A North Carolina regiment mistook his group and assumed it was an attack by Federal forces. They opened fire at close range. Stonewall Jackson was hit three times – in the right hand, left wrist and upper left arm where an artery was severed.

That night his left arm was amputated at the shoulder. While still conscious in bed for several days he had asked for updates on the battle with special inquiries for his old brigade who he learned had gallantly charged even over the backs of other confederates and driven the Yankees from behind their breast works. "It was just like them" Jackson responded "they are a noble set of men. The name Stonewall belongs to that brigade, not to me." 4

By Sunday, May 10th he was delirious with fever and pneumonia, babbling orders and speaking to his imagined wife and child. His reported last words were "Let us cross over the river and rest under the shades of the trees."

John O. Casler later wrote: "The news of the wounding of General Jackson filled the army with the most profound and undisguised grief. His men loved him devotedly, and he was the idol of the whole army. Many stout hearted veterans who had under his guidance borne hardships and privations innumerable, and dangers the most appalling without a murmur, wept like children when told their idolized general was no more." 5

Stonewall Jackson exemplified the strength and ambition of the Confederacy. His death was its spiritual climax. Never again would the tide of Confederate hopes and victories rise as high as they had heretofore. The aftermath of the battle of Chancellorsville was traumatic for the Union with more than 17,000 casualties to the Confederates' 13,000. Lincoln exclaimed "My God! My God! What will the country say?" Hooker had been completely mastered by Lee whose deification across the South was now complete. Chancellorsville went down as his most dazzling victory.

Lee now planned a second invasion of the North hoping to demoralize it with the ravishes of war, stroke the anti war sentiments of the Union, negotiate a troop exchange and possible peace settlement, gain European recognition and find provisions that his poorly fed and clothed men desperately needed.

After Chancellorsville, the Stonewall Brigade, some without shoes, began the long march through the Shenandoah Valley to Gettysburg (*Century Magazine*)

20

Gettysburg

"If I had Stonewall Jackson at Gettysburg I would have won that fight and a complete victory would have given us Washington and Baltimore, if not Philadelphia and would have established the independency of the Confederacy."

Robert E. Lee

Following Chancellorville, the Confederate army was given a full month to rest, recuperate and gather supplies. On June 10th the Stonewall Brigade, now under the leadership of Richard Ewell, moved home into the Shenandoah Valley amidst the cheers of their families at Berryville and elsewhere hoping to be liberated anew from Yankee occupation. That they were!

In the second battle of Winchester (June 13 – 15 1863) thanks in large part to the Stonewall Brigade, who suffered only 38 casualties and 3 deaths to the Union's 450 dead and wounded and 4,000 missing or captured, Ewell captured 23 guns, 300 loaded wagons, hundreds of horses and a huge amount of supplies before joining Confederate forces spreading across southern Pennsylvania, plundering as they went, and finally assembling near a small town named Gettysburg.

It was here on July 1 – 3, 1863, that Robert E. Lee and the Confederacy suffered a stunning defeat and both sides showed courage that defies human imagination. 23,000 Union men and 28,000 Confederates, almost one third of the total number, were killed, wounded or missing after the three days of fighting. 7,000 Confederate soldiers were too badly wounded to remove and were left behind. The Stonewall Brigade lost a third of its members (318 men) despite the fact that, for the most part, they were stationed on the outskirts of the conflict. The first instinct throughout the South, which has evolved through analysis and scholarship even to this day, is that if Stonewall Jackson had been alive at Gettysburg the Confederates would have found a way to win.

General Meade reported to Abraham Lincoln that he had driven "from our soil every vestige of the presence of the intruder." "My God is that all?" cried Lincoln, who wanted and expected the destruction of Lee and his weakened army as they retreated across the Potomac, back into Virginia, where Lee would regroup to fight for nearly two more years.

Lee felt that he had some element of success. He brought back with him gigantic trains of supplies in addition to large quantities of food that the Confederacy would otherwise have had to pay for, removed the immediate threat to the capitol, Richmond, and did great damage to Northern forces.

21

THE BATTLE OF MINE RUN

After the battle of Gettysburg, General Robert E. Lee's Army of Northern Virginia and Major General George Meade's Army of the Potomac returned to Virginia and fought a series of smaller engagements. The Mine Run campaign was the last of these battles before both sides settled into winter camp.

In-mid November 1863, Meade, with his army of roughly 80,000 men to Lee's 50,000, encamped south of the Rapidan River and learned that the right positions of Lee's army were unguarded. He formulated a plan that would depend on "prompt vigorous action and intelligent compliance on the part of his officers." [1] His plan was to pass by the unguarded positions and attack Lee from the rear.

John Michael Pope and the Stonewall Brigade were camped near Fredericksburg by a stream called Mine Run awaiting a battle at any moment. Lee and a number of his staff officers were riding down the line of battle when they came upon a party of soldiers engaged in prayer. Already the sharp shooting for the upcoming battle had begun along the skirmish line and the artillery had just begun to fire. When Lee saw these men, however, he immediately dismounted and, uncovering his head, joined them in prayer. The rest of his staff followed the example of their chieftain. One can only imagine the surprise of the enlisted men (most likely John Michael included) when prayers were finished to find that they had just led their beloved commander before the throne of grace. [2]

Meade planned to launch his campaign on November 24th but heavy rains caused a 48 hour delay and although Lee did not know Meade's intent he did know that the Federals were about to move. On November 26th muddy roads slowed Meade's advance and Lee shifted his army east in an effort to block Meade's flanking maneuver. Daybreak on the 27th found both sides moving towards each other. At about 4 p.m. a major battle took place at Payne Farm where 32,000 Union soldiers came up against Major General Edward Johnson with 5,300 veterans including the Stonewall Brigade.

Here the heaviest fighting of the campaign occurred as troops charged and counter-charged across the fields of Payne Farm and into the adjacent woods. Here John Michael Pope became a casualty of the Civil War being wounded in the right shoulder. After dark, the Confederates pulled back to a new position on high ground and strengthened the position by constructing strong earthworks. Meade's plan had failed and heavy rains and muddy roads again hampered further advance. On November 29th Meade had hoped to make a final attack and was ready to do so around 5 p.m. but darkness foiled this plan.

Overnight the temperature dropped below freezing and without tents, shelters or even fires, the soldiers went through what for many was perhaps the worst night of the war. Frustrated by Lee's counter-moves, low on provisions and faced with continuing bad weather, Meade retreated on December 1st. After lying wounded for two days in the freezing weather, John Michael Pope was finally transferred to the Confederate hospital Chimborazo at Richmond. Lee always regretted the inconclusive results of this battle. He is quoted as saying "I am too old to command this army. We never should have permitted these people to get away." With Confederate hopes of a repeat of their Chancellorsville triumph dashed, Lee withdrew into winter quarters.

22

CHIMBORAZO

"Like the dim caverns of the catacombs where instead of the dead in their final rest, there were wasted figures burning with fever and raving from the agony of splintered bones, tossing restlessly from side to side with every ill it seemed, which human flesh was heir to. From the rafters the flickering oil lamp swung mournfully, casting a ghastly light upon the scene beneath."

Pvt. Alexander Hunter, 17th Virginia Infantry

Several million men took up arms during the Civil War. They fell sick in unprecedented numbers and died from wounds and disease by the hundreds of thousands. The sudden burden of caring for so many men resulted in hundreds of hospitals sprouting up. This was true in the South particularly around the city of Richmond with its proximity to many of the war's greatest battles and its location at the junction of five converging railroads. Ironically, one makeshift hospital was set up in Berryville at the Showers' house where John Michael came of age

No medical facility North or South equaled the fame and notoriety of the one to which John Michael was first taken – Chimborazo. It was located on a hill in the eastern end of Richmond and named for an inactive volcano in Ecuador 21,000 feet in elevation. Of the 34 military hospitals in Richmond, Chimborazo quickly emerged as one of the largest, best organized and most sophisticated hospitals in the Confederacy. "Over crowding, however, combined with short supplies and inadequate personnel, produced a medical hell … it became infamous for its odors. The putrid smell of gangrene mixed with the stench of suppurating wounds and the foul aromas of torn flesh trying to heal. Piles of duty rags littered floors wet from blood and water. Shortages of soap left bedding and patients' clothing perpetually filthy. The limited number of mattresses and blankets were used over and over again until they rotted." [1]

Chimborazo's personnel were also unlike anything ever seen before. In addition to the dozens of physicians who were organized into a hierarchy of ranked surgeons, the hospital employed enormous nursing and support staffs. Military hospitals had previously been manned largely by convalescing soldiers, but the labor needs at Chimborazo were so great, as was the pressure for any able soldiers to return to the front, that it was forced to rely heavily on slaves, free blacks and white women to keep it running. About 1,000 women served in Confederate hospitals compared to 9,000 in the North primarily because the use of hired out male slaves in the South preempted the recruitment of white women.

John Michael Pope was hospitalized there on November 30, 1863. On January 18, 1864 he was hospitalized at Staunton, Virginia and again on June 25th at Charlottesville, Virginia. On July 16, 1864, he returned to duty some eight months before the Civil War was to end.

23

ON THE HOME FRONT

"While it was Grant who initially ordered Sheridan to turn the Shenandoah into a barren wasteland, it was Sherman alone who first glimpsed the true meaning of the maelstrom of total war ... attacking villages, cities ...creating not just outright death, but long lines of starving refugees ... hitting livestock, food, private homes, plantations ... shops ... telegraph wires ... It was terror ..." [1]

"One old gentleman, while his barns were burning, sat on his front porch and sang Let the Yankees burn what they will, we'll be gay and happy still." [2]

The Civil War profoundly affected Berryville and surrounding towns. Personal property was stolen, citizens were shot and murdered, homes illegally occupied and destroyed. Berryville was part of the Shenandoah Valley that was known as the "bread basket of the Confederacy." Agricultural pursuits were so destroyed that Union General Philip Sheridan, who laid waste the area in 1864, proclaimed that "the crow that flies over the Valley of Virginia must henceforth carry his rations with him."

During the war nearby Winchester changed hands as many as 72 times, 13 times in one day. One of the most notable actions during the Civil War occurred when John Singleton Mosby and his guerrilla band raided General Philip Sheridan's seven mile long supply train in Berryville.

Treadwell Smith of Berryville kept a detailed diary from October 17, 1859 to April 20, 1865. Smith's diary provides us with an excellent outline of this period in Berryville history and offers valuable insight into the plight of Berryville's citizens, including the Pope family.

It was not until March 10, 1862, that the Federal armies moved from Charles Town into Berryville. Many residents evacuated only to return to try to make the best of it enduring all kinds of suffering and trials including a serious threat of the town being burned. This was sometime after the battle of Kernstown.

Conrad Pope, Michael Pope, Jr. and sister Barbara Greenwald were all farming at this particular point in the area around Stone's Chapel, and Kilian (1823 – 1880), the grandson of Johann Popp and a stone mason, was living near Winchester in the area known as Shawnee. None of the men served in the Confederate army and all three, at one time or another, suffered at the hands of Union forces.

Conrad (1821 – 1895) and Michael (1828 – 1914) had married sisters, daughters of Conrad and Olivia (Mercer) Swarz. While their father was decidedly German, the ancestors of the sisters' mother, Olivia, were apparently English Quakers. It might have been this influence that kept their husbands from war, but that is speculation. Michael and Mary Swartz had at least eight children and Conrad and his wife, Elizabeth Swartz, had at least eight also.

In 1861, Conrad would have been 40 years of age. The choice of names for the children seems to indicate a certain bent to American patriotism. These include E. Washington Pope (1843 – 1864) and Benjamin Franklin Pope (1842 – 1914). In the case of E. Washington, he was in the 2nd Virginia Infantry Stonewall Brigade with John Michael. After a rough start (he intentionally broke his gunstock sometime before June 30, 1861) he was wounded in battle and hospitalized at the Confederate General Hospital on April 26, 1863, and released returning to service on May 8th. He was captured July 17, 1864 (the day after John Michael Pope returned to service) and died of typhoid fever in Yankee prison at Camp Chase, Ohio on December 23, 1864, at the age of 21, about five months before the war's end.

Another one of Conrad's sons, William, born in 1841, enlisted on June 6, 1861, at Camp Jackson on Bolivar Heights. He was wounded at the First Battle of Winchester. On February 9, 1863, he was a prisoner of war (Wheeling Camp Chase, West Virginia) and was exchanged on March 28, 1863. He was hospitalized at Staunton, returning in July and August. William was again taken as a prisoner of war at Spotsylvania, held at Fort Lookout in Elmira, New York, and released on June 1, 1865.

Michael Pope is referred to any number of times in documents of the period and especially during the summer of 1864 when Sheridan ravished the area in which the family lived. At one point, all the men of the area aged 16 and upward were arrested and loaded in wagon trains or force marched to Shepherds Town for eventual imprisonment. This round up included Michael Pope and Frank Pope. Fortunately, after 48 hours, the Yankee officer in charge said that he would release them if they took the oath of allegiance to the Federal government which they all did except for Thomas Jones (1817 – 1899) who stated that he had sons in the Confederate army, was in sympathy with the cause and would aide them whenever he could. "The officer said he did not blame him and under the same circumstances he would do likewise, and if the other gentlemen would say that … he was a peaceable citizen and did not belong to Mosby's Band he would let him go." [3]

The fate of roundup and imprisonment during this period fell to Kilian Pope, son of Maria Annah (b. 1800) Johann Michael's daughter. His mother immigrated in 1842. Kilian did not get off so easily during the summer of 1864. Under the orders of General Grant a number of male citizens liable for conscription were arrested. Among them were Kilian Pope and James Forster. (I had communicated with Forster's daughter in 1963). They were imprisoned in Fort McHenry until they were released a number of months later through the efforts of Confederate sympathizers in Baltimore.

After his Chancellorville victory, General Robert E. Lee's army headed north in June of 1863 bound for Pennsylvania where he hoped to fight a decisive battle that would produce southern nationhood. Headquartered under a large oak just north of Berryville on Sunday, June 21st, Lee attended services at the Episcopal church in Berryville with a number of his officers including General James Longstreet. They would meet again in defeat at Gettysburg.

From the time the militia was called out in 1861 throughout the war many of the larger slave-owning farms in the Shenandoah Valley were left to be run by the older men, the women and the slaves. When the Union forces moved in, many of the slaves availed themselves of the first chance to leave for Pennsylvania and freedom.

Characteristically, on August 16, 1862 Treadwell Smith notes that a number of slaves went to "the land of freedom." The following January he reports that he got one of his own back paying Captain S. R. Jackson $50 to go after him. [4] Lincoln's arming of African Americans and the Emancipation Proclamation (January 1, 1863) helped spur an estimated one million slaves to escape to the North.

It is interesting to note that some Southerners had, as early as 1861, been talking about arming and emancipating the slaves. Back home in Berryville, Clarke County and throughout the South slaves were used in great numbers to support the Confederacy, transporting and loading supplies, constructing fortifications, digging trenches, cooking and serving food in hospitals, burying the dead and all sorts of forms of back breaking drudgery. Free blacks in some instances rallied to the Confederate cause, some even offering themselves as soldiers.

It was during the summer of 1864, around the time of Kilian Pope's imprisonment and John Michael Pope's return to service, that the people of Clarke County and the South were forced to realize that they were going to have to choose between slavery and independence. After four years of private debate and two years of public debate, on March 13th, with the support of Robert E. Lee and President Jefferson Davis, the Confederate congress passed a bill calling for the enlistment of 300,000 black men with the right of freedom after their service granted to all those who enlist. Blacks were to be in integrated regiments unlike the North. Nathan Burwell of Clarke County was one of many soldiers and slave owners who came forward pledging to form companies of blacks. [5]

Throughout the war many friends of the Pope family were to suffer. On August 18, 1864, the house of Province McCormick, and its entire contents, were burned to the ground per order of General George Custer. The period of the war with the most action for the town of Berryville appears to have been in this time frame and included the Battle of Cool Spring on July 17 and 18, 1864 (the Union army following Jubal Early back from his raid on Washington), the Buck Marsh Fight on August 13, 1864 (Mosby's attack on Sheridan's wagon train), the Battle of Berryville on September 3, 1864, in which Union forces were literally driven out of town, and the Fight at Gold's Farm which took place on the same date. There was also a skirmish at Stone's Chapel.

John S. Mosby and Men

Records indicate that John Michael Pope had an acquaintance with the dashing, slight in stature John Singleton Mosby (1833 – 1916) who is shown here with feather in cap surrounded by his men of the 43rd Battalion First Virginia Cavalry known as Mosby's Rangers or Raiders, a partisan ranger unit known for its lightening quick raids and its ability to elude the Union army and disappear blending in with local farmers and townsmen in Berryville and throughout the Shenandoah Valley. "Mosby knew that if his raiders had a camp it would sooner or later lead to their capture. Instead, he appealed to patriotic Virginians, whose men folk were away in the army and whose slaves were running away, to board his men in their houses much to the delight of numerous teenaged girls who desperately fanning themselves felt [their] young hearts go pitter pat." [6]

An attorney and man of letters opposed to slavery, Mosby's guerrilla warfare that bolstered Southern spirits was also extremely successful. The Union was forced to keep upwards of 30,000 men in the area to defend its interests. Large numbers of young men were attracted to his band's free and easy life with its opportunities for plunder as they were allowed to take anything of value on their prisoners including large sums of money that they divided amongst themselves.

In August of 1864, just outside of Berryville on present day Route 7, Mosby attacked one of Sheridan's wagon trains capturing 75 wagons, 200 beef cattle, 600 horses and mules and 200 prisoners. On September 22nd 1864, Sheridan executed 6 of Mosby's men in retaliation and Mosby retaliated likewise. Shortly thereafter they reached a truce on such executions.

After the war, Mosby was campaign manager for Ulysses S. Grant who became a personal friend. He became a great reconciler between North and South and held many government positions.

24

WAR'S FINAL DAYS

"... what now struck Lee was the destitution of his beloved army. There were no shoes, no overcoats no blankets and little food; men scrambled between the legs of horses for dung to sift for undigested corn. There was insanity, exhaustion, wounds gone gangrenous. ... Lee had 35,000 men present for duty ... Grant ... the Union commander would [soon] ... have 280,000." [1]

Death, honor, valor, desperation and hunger - these were the realities of the final days of the Confederacy. As a nation, it had shriveled to parts of Virginia, North and South Carolina along with small areas further south and in Mississippi. John Michael Pope returns to his brigade on July 16, 1864, about 9 months before the surrender of Robert E. Lee. During the time period leading up to April, 1865, he is caught up in the final desperate days of the Confederacy.

By the time John Michael returns, the Stonewall Brigade is reduced to the size of less than a normal regiment and it was merged into a consolidated brigade of Virginians. The remaining Stonewall veterans, however, stayed together and maintained their identity. At the time of his return, John Michael's brigade was close to home in the Shenandoah Valley and he most likely participated in the third Battle of Winchester on September 19, 1864 and on October 18th at Cedar Creek, 20 miles south of Winchester. After this latest defeat, over 1,000 Confederates were captured and many simply abandoned their ranks.

In December, 1864 the Brigade, or Second Corps, was called back to Petersburg to participate in the siege. Cold, hungry and under constant fire, the remaining Stonewallers shared trenches with the rest of the Army of Northern Virginia, at first on the Confederate right but later toward the center.

On March 25, 1865 Lee tried unsuccessfully to break the siege. By April 1st the town of Petersburg was no longer tenable and neither was the capitol, Richmond. Lee told Jefferson Davis that the capitol had to be evacuated the next day. On April 2nd the Army of Northern Virginia began its last march along the Appomatox River with the remainder of the Stonewall Brigade as rear guard. Most of the Second Corps was cut off and captured and, finally, all of the starving Virginians had the line of retreat blocked by the Federals.

On April 9, 1865 Lee met Grant at Appomattox Court House and surrendered the Army of Northern Virginia. All that Grant asked was that the Confederates surrender their weapons and return to their homes. Mounted men were allowed to keep their horses. Federal troops came forward outside the Court House to share their rations with the starved Confederates.

On April 12, 1865 the final ceremony took place as the Army of Northern Virginia stacked its flag and arms. The few survivors of the Stonewall Brigade were given the honor of leading the final march. Union soldiers stood in solid ranks and solemnly pressed arms in salute. Out of the approximately 6,000 men who served in the Stonewall Brigade during the course of the Civil War, only 210 remained at the time of the surrender. It is most likely that John Michael Pope was not present at the surrender as he was paroled on April 13th at Winchester. Treadwell Smith notes in his diary two days later that John Michael gave himself up that morning along with 5 other Confederates. On April 20th Smith notes that the Yankees "pulled up stakes and left." [2]

And so the war was over and John Michael Pope, cited for distinguished service, was home at Berryville. Over 620,000 lay dead, one twelfth of the total population of the North and one fifth of the South, numbers so staggering that they almost stop meaning anything. Southerners were "incoherent with grief, their land diseased and without cure." [3]

In his book *April 1865*, Jay Winik tells us that the only way to appreciate the full magnitude of the South's wholesale devastation is to reverse the Southern names on to Northern cities: New York, Chicago, Boston, Philadelphia, Washington, Concord and, yes, even New Haven burned to the ground, Westpoint ransacked and torched, The New York Times, the Baltimore Sun and the Boston Globe shut down, Princeton and Yale closed and the careers of folk like Walt Whitman, Emily Dickinson, Nathaniel Hawthorne, Teddy Roosevelt, Henry Ford and P.T. Barnum cut short.

Winik points out that the names, of course, were Southern and included Berryville and the Shenandoah Valley. Here towns and cities and the countryside had experienced Sherman's guerrilla warfare bringing on terror and death. Livestock, food, homes, shops, railroads and telegraph wires had been destroyed. Men made the way home to Berryville and Clarke County, often on foot and depending on the impoverished along the way for food. "Before them work, hard work but they went at it bravely as they had gone at their old enemy." [4]

"Their contributions in the years that followed were to be many as they labored to build a new south through hard work, providing stable political leadership preserving history, securing veterans benefits and advocating national reconciliation." [5]

TRIBUTE TO THE CONFEDERATE SOLDIERS
by John O. Crown

Oh, warrior children of a war-torn land,
Who carved Confederate fame on heights so grand –
Who bathed your battle standards in the glory
That shines adown the aisles of classic story –
Who reared your valorous deeds in Alps that rise
O'er sad defeat to shine in Honor's skies;
Ah, me; that after all the gifts you gave,
That garland only your lost nation's grave.

Grandly, Oh Southern nation, dawned the morn,
When, helmeted with hope and battle-born,
You girt your land with saber strokes, the pour
Of leaden rain, and cannons' thundering roar.
Your midday splendor, flashing wide and high,
Led our brave thoughts to soar in faith's sweet sky,
And all our struggles melted in a dream
Of victory and peace by freedom's stream.

Alas, then came defeat's sad woeful night,
When all our grand achievements pass'd from sight,
To reappear a World Force nevermore
By hill and vale, and stream, and wave-washed shore;
When swords were sheath'd, and war-drums ceased to beat,
And bannerless you plod with weary feet
Into the deepening gloom of the unknown,
Where vanquish'd wander when hope's stars are gone.

Oh, men once marshal'd by the matchless Lee,
Or march'd with "Stonewall's band" to victory –
Oh, men who follow'd Hampton's waving plume,
Or saw the gallant Stuart meet his doom –
Oh, men who climb'd the heights all cannon-crown'd
Though death with fire and thunder rock'd the ground,
The Warriors of the World rein in their steeds,
And with admiring gaze salute your deeds.

Fair, sunny land, where strove the hero-hearted.
Woe toll'd from all our joy-bells when we parted
With our loved banner on that fatal field
That saw your martial strength to starving yield;
While seas are rock'd by storms and mountains stand,
And thought ascends to realms where words are grand,
Your fame shall stream across the wide world's pages –
Ride down in glory through the far-flung ages.

John Crown of the Clarke County Courier wrote this piece as a tribute to the Confederate soldier. It captures the nationalistic spirit embraced by John Michael Pope and the Confederacy.

The Lost Cause

This print was created for the southern market by Currier and Ives. It depicts the return of a Confederate veteran to his abandoned homestead where he encounters the graves of his wife and child. The sun is setting in the background symbolizing the descent of southern independence with the Confederate flag rising over the headstones appearing in the form of a cross reminding us that once it was lost the cause became holy.

25

FAMILY AT HOME

Following the Civil War, Berryville returned to normalcy. The large carriage shops were reopened as well as several banks. New stores opened and a thriving building association was organized.

In 1880 the Shenandoah Valley Railroad was finished with Berryville becoming one of its most important stations handling a high volume of freight and passenger traffic. The Berryville Flour Milling Company was established and wheat and corn were joined by prosperous horse farms and apple orchards to name just a few of the diversified agricultural pursuits.

The United States Census of 1870 finds John Michael Pope back in Berryville living on East Main Street in a house he purchased in 1868 and successfully in business as a tailor. He was married three years earlier on August 8, 1867 to Harriet Hamilton (b. June 26, 1848 at Preston, Virginia). Harriet was a woman of Scotch-Irish descent known for her remarkable piety and was a much sought–after dressmaker. The couple is a shining example of the Methodist evangelical piety that dominates the period. Pasted in the front cover of their Bible (American Tract Society 1852) is an 1874 list of all the appointments of ministers to churches in the Baltimore District Southern Methodist Conference. The list includes the appointment of S. Townshend (for whom their only son and my grandfather, Arthur Townshend, was to be named) to the Duncan Memorial Church at Berryville.

At home is one daughter, Esther Lee, who was born on August 25, 1868. The promise to Robert E. Lee had been kept. Also in the household was Annie Greenwalt, age 22, and Elizabeth Clink, age 61. Annie Greenwalt is presumably the daughter of Adam and Barbara (Babette) Popp Greenwalt and niece of John Michael.

Elizabeth Clink, known as Miss Betsy, can be found in Berryville history prior to 1850 living in a one story long house on Main Street. "She was a little old lady living alone and made a great deal over children. Everybody liked Miss Betsy and helped her in any way that they could. She made lots of mending and darning for people. She never would make a charge, but everyone gave her something. Her eye sight got so bad she could not thread her needles and they had to be threaded for her. She used to call children in to do little turns for her and always gave them cookies." [1]

In the 1850 U. S. Census Elizabeth Clink is age 40 and a member of the household of Joseph and Mary Noble on Main Street. As we have noted, they were also Methodists and the incorporating of Miss Betsy in the household by both the Nobles and the Popes surely was an outgrowth of their Methodist piety of "encouraging the faint hearted and supporting the weak."

There is commerce in the area where the Popes are living including not only John Michael's tailor shop but also a blacksmith shop, a sumac and bark mill, a wagon maker, oyster saloon, tin ware, shoes and cigar merchants. Nearby lives Matthew Pulliam, the wagon maker, who was in business in Berryville for 64 years and known by every man, woman and child in the County. He was the first Mayor of Berryville and served three one year terms. He was a man of tremendous physical vigor and strength. Pulliam had also lived in the House on the Rock where John Michael had first opened his tailor shop in 1858. He was drafted into service twice during the Civil War. At one point Stonewall Jackson himself ordered him back to Berryville saying that "such a man was worth more to his country at home making wagons than in the army."

Looking East on Main Street, Berryville about 1890
Photograph courtesy of Clarke County Historical Association

Here, in the heart of town, is where the charmed life of the Pope family was lived. However, research reveals that, like many Virginia towns, Berryville practiced a form of apartheid that descended as a dark cloud after the abolition of slavery.

As we have seen, prior to the Civil War enslaved blacks made up 55 percent of the population of Clarke County. They were held under strict control on large plantations outside of Berryville, but many town residents also owned slaves.

"Immediately after the war they stayed on and sharecropped. But the going was hard, and they found it difficult to deal with the overall atmosphere in a place where they had been slaves … many moved to Ohio, Pennsylvania and Canada taking with them skills as masons and iron workers that they learned here." [2] Those who stayed were subject to strict Virginia segregation laws.

After the Civil War, African Americans were free but not equal. The Civil Rights Acts of 1866 and 1875 and the Fourteenth and Fifteenth Amendments to the United States Constitution were made dead issues by hostile court decisions culminating in 1896 in *Plessy v. Ferguson* that gave legal sanction to separate but equal facilities. However, these laws were based on the ideas expressed in the Supreme Court's *Dred Scott* decision of 1857 that blacks were an "inferior and subordinate class of beings." This remained the attitude of most whites and governments. Jim Crow, taking its name from a fictional minstrel character, was the name given to America's own system of racial apartheid. Although Virginia gained a reputation for relatively harmonious race relations (compared to other southern states), it enacted 25 Jim Crow laws from 1870 to 1960. These were not repealed until passage of the Civil Rights Act of 1964.

"These laws also known as black codes were also enacted to ease southerners' fears that formerly enslaved persons would attack them as revenge for slavery and to ensure a continued supply of cheap or even free labor, reducing blacks to legal servitude similar to and in some cases worse than slavery." [3]

In Virginia, the South, and in some northern states, blacks had to sit at the back of street cars and stand when there was not enough room for whites. They were made to sit in separate sections of theaters, libraries and train stations. They could not use water fountains, bathrooms, beaches or swimming pools used by whites. They could only order take out food from restaurants that served whites and that had to be picked up from the back door. They attended separate, usually ramshackle, schools. Social life and everything from sports teams to funeral parlors was segregated. Northern segregation was de facto and its patterns were housing enforced by covenants, bank lending practices, and discriminatory job and union practices.

After the Civil War, blacks developed some 20 communities in Clarke County. "Many of these were established in the 1870s by former slaves who had purchased land at auction from financially strapped whites – often at the edge of existing communities – and then subdivided the land selling to others of their race…" [4]

One such community, not far from the hub of Main Street and the Pope residence, was Josephine City comprising 31 acres. The land was originally part of Clermont, a 355 acre plantation granted by Lord Fairfax of Cameron to John Vance in 1751 and inherited by Edward McCormick in 1834. Following McCormick's death and the Civil War, his widow, Ellen, deeply in debt, twice failed to sell the land at public auction to whites. She then subdivided the property and sold the lots to her former slave Josephine (who had now become a successful seamstress in town) and another 16 black families.

A self sufficient community, Josephine City came to include a school, grocery store, barber shops, gas station, boarding houses, restaurant, cemetery, two churches, milliner's shop and meat market.

Thomas Gold, in his *History of Clarke County*, praises the settlement of Josephine City but, in his discussion of both slavery and the period after the war, always writes from the point of view that blacks are separate from white society and even goes so far as to state that "as a class the Negro (under slavery) was more comfortable, better clad and better fed than now in his freedom ..." [5]

The Pope family, like most white residents of Clarke County, appears to have had little or no social intercourse with the black community, and their Methodist piety of social support and reform did not seem to extend to that population. Indeed, even in the present day, Methodists remain somewhat separate both north and south owing to the presence of the African American Methodist Episcopal Church denomination that merges the Wesleyan tradition with African heritage.

The J. M. Pope family continues to grow in this period with Hannah Showers Pope being born in 1872, Ursula Virginia in 1874 and Arthur Townsend in 1883.

John Michael Pope

Harriet Hamilton Pope

26

Esther Lee Pope

Esther Lee Pope, John Michael and Harriet's first child, was born in 1868 and died at age 22. In a letter written a few months before she died there are complaints of a severe headache and it was often speculated that she may have had some neurological problems. Her photograph depicts a beautiful young woman and her letters home to her sister Hannah from Front Royal detail the life and interests of a typical young woman in post Civil War Virginia.

In his moving play *Our Town,* Thornton Wilder immortalized forever the universality of the average unexceptional life of a young girl growing up in a small American town at the turn of the 20th century. While the play is set in New Hampshire, it could be anywhere in America.

I always think of Emily, Wilder's main character, when I think of Esther Lee. After dying in childbirth, Emily is given the opportunity to return to Earth for a brief time. Before returning to her grave, she pauses for one more look at life and exclaims:

"I didn't realize so all that was going on and we never noticed … Wait! One more look, good-bye, good-bye world, good-bye Grovers Corners … Mama and Papa. Good-bye to clocks ticking … and Mama's sunflowers, and food and coffee. And new ironed dresses and hot baths … and sleeping and waking up. Oh Earth you're too wonderful for anyone to realize you …"[1]

How like Emily was Esther Lee. In a December 30, 1889 letter from Front Royal where the family spent some time, she writes to sister Hannah "I know you didn't miss me as much as I do you, but I won't let anybody see me cry." She talks of Papa's cough and her little brother Arthur's cold and facets of church life including the fact that their minister is rather "dry." She talks of various other "entertainments" and social events in town. There is quite a bit of gossip about boys and of peers being married including one named Riddle of whom she quips "I pity the girl that would have him."

Evidently there was quite a bit of family contact for she mentions her family at Berryville extensively, complaining that they have not written. Like young girls today on social media, she expresses that she is lonesome and has a strong need to fit in.

She is quite clothes conscious, expressing the fact that "Mama is making Emma J. such a lovely tea gown. Just wish I could have one like it." She also promises to send a piece of another dress in progress for Hannah to look at.

Esther reads a great deal and apparently is involved in housekeeping with several "boarders" who "do not eat much." She closes a letter saying that she has just read Chapter One of *Opening a Chestnut Burr*. She is quite alarmed by the chapter, writing "it had such a strange affect on me that I don't feel like I want to read another one." The author is E. P. Roe (1838 – 1888), a Presbyterian minister whose popular American novels outsold those of Mark Twain. Harpers Magazine had called him "thoroughly religious, thoroughly Christian in tone and teaching."

Of the main character in *Opening a Chestnut Burr*, the Atlantic Monthly wrote that it was a tale of a "selfish, morbid cynical hero and his gradual transformation under the influence of a sweet and high spirited heroine who the New York Tribune states 'is a model of saintly purpose and ardent piety without losing the peculiar charms of female loveliness.'"

This sounds a bit like Esther Lee herself, but I understand why she was so alarmed by the first chapter where she learned that the hero "believed that with few exceptions men and women lived for their own profit and pleasure, and that religion and creeds were matters of custom and fashion, or an accident of birth." This was, of course, contrary to everything Esther believed.

Nevertheless, her citing the novel and her brief comments about it open a very large window into the life and times of young men and women in the post Civil War period. Ironically, *Opening a Chestnut Burr* is now a free Kindle book and is also available as a reprint on Amazon.

Esther Lee rests with her parents and two sisters in the Green Hill Cemetery at Berryville.

Esther Lee Pope

27

Hannah Showers Pope and George J. Cunningham, Sr.

"Miss Hannah was my Sunday School teacher for many years and a very fine spiritual teacher. I used to go to Miss Hannah to talk over problems with her and get her advice. It was always a great satisfaction."

Mrs. Hugh G. (Edna) Owens

"Berryville paid tribute to the memory of the late George Cunningham, for years a beloved citizen, when funeral services were held from the Methodist church. At that hour business was at a standstill ... as they closed their doors and pulled down the shutters as a mark of respect to this good man. The entire community gathered at the church to pay respect to this good man."

Winchester Evening Star
April 14, 1919

Hannah Showers Pope was born on June 7, 1872. She was named for Hannah Showers who, together with her husband, Manuel, had raised her father, John Michael. Presentation book awards found in the trunk in the attic in New Haven given by Berryville High School for "Scholarship and Deportment" as well as some of Hannah's compositions reveal a talent for writing and a solid evangelical Methodist faith. Career opportunities for young women were not readily available and it appears that, aside from her church work, Hannah pretty much devoted herself to keeping the family home, both with her parents and later in her marriage.

On November 27, 1907, at the age of 35 she married 57 year old George J. Cunningham, Sr., a Methodist layman and one of the most highly regarded men in Berryville. George was of Irish descent and his father, Francis Marion Cunningham, who was a twin, fought with the Confederate army. The wedding took place at 8:30 in the morning in the Methodist parsonage followed by a short honeymoon in Washington D.C.

George's first wife was Elizabeth Eddy of Winchester, Virginia. They had three children. Elizabeth Eddy's father operated the Valley Mills at Abrams Creek east of Winchester. George became the owner of the mills and adjoining farm after Mr. Eddy's death.

A miller all his life, George Cunningham's father, Marion Cunningham, operated a mill at Marlboro where George worked as a youth before moving to Winchester to work at W.B. Bakers Sons, one of the largest roller flour mills in the state.

Upon moving to Berryville, he became the manager of the Berryville Milling Company where, as noted in one of his obituaries, "Notwithstanding the fact that the mill has changed hands a number of times every new management which came in retained Mr. Cunningham. He had developed the art of making flour with modern machinery as he had with old time burrs."

Shortly after George came to Berryville he was made superintendent of the Methodist Church Sunday School which thrived under his leadership. Upon his retirement, three weeks after a stroke, he was presented with a silver service and $30 in gold. The presentation card was in the trunk in the attic in New Haven. Of his faith and life as a leader in the Methodist church his obituary notes:

"He was a high toned Christian and a splendid type of citizen who sought to do good in a quiet and unostentatious way." Shortly after his death, the Duncan Memorial Church passed a resolution that read in part: "Be it resolved then that in Brother George J. Cunningham's life the Church and man and God, we believe had a loyal friend, and today he being dead yet speaketh. His name shall be enshrined in the annals of this church and his memory with us shall be an immortelle of the grace of God and a human life."

I have always thought that there must have been a lovely story surrounding the courtship and marriage of Hannah and George. They had twelve happy years together.

Hannah Showers Pope

George J. Cunningham
"Be it resolved then that in Brother George J. Cunningham's life the Church and man and God, we believe had a loyal friend, and today he being dead yet speaketh. His name shall be enshrined in the annals of this church and his memory with us shall be an immortelle of the grace of God and a human life."
Portion of a Resolution of the Duncan Memorial Methodist Church, Berryville, VA
April 5, 1920

DOWN IN THE MIRE
By Hannah Pope

Down in the slush and the mud of the street,
Kicked on one side by the passenger's feet,
Hat battered in and eyes flashing fire,
Headlong the drunkard falls down in the mire.

Bus drivers shout as he staggers along,
Yelling the chorus of some filthy song,
With his hoarse voice rising higher and higher,
But now he has fallen down into the mire.

Boys selling boxo' lights yell at his heels,
Stones fly fast at him as onward he reels,
A crowd gathers round and asks "Is it fire?"
No it is only a drunken man down in the mire.

Young maidens with curls like bright threads of pure gold,
Forgive me fair maidens, if I am too bold,
You have health, you have beauty, & all you desire,
Just look for one moment down in the mire.

You have lovers in plenty who sigh at your feet,
But there's one and one only whose whisper is sweet,
'Tis right you should love him, but lady come nigher,
He was somebody's lover once, that man in the mire.

Foot passengers stop, ere you pass on your way,
Don't tell me you're awfully busy today,
You have put down your name to build a church spire,
Here's a broken down temple down in the mire.

Ruddy cheeked boy on your way to the school,
Cramming your head with hard science by rule,
Don't think that book learning is all you require,
Here's a lesson for you my boy down in the mire.

Don't open your blue eyes so wide on me now,
Don't curl up your lip and wrinkle your brow,
He once was a schoolboy, with heart full of fire,
But now, he lies helpless down in the mire.

Ladies shrink from him and shudder with fear,
Lest the poor drunkard should stagger too near
Drawing still closer their silken attire,
Lest he should spatter their clothing with mire.

Little girl, little girl singing blithely with glee,
Just stay for one moment and listen to me,
When you bring pappa's slippers to warm at the fire,
Think of somebody's father who's down in the mire.

Yes somebody's father is down in the street,
Kicked on one side by the passenger's feet
Hat battered in and eyes flashing fire
Yelling out curses while down in the mire.

Will nobody help him? Will nobody save?
This poor stranded wreck on life's troubled wave,
Yes, yes we will struggle to lift him up higher,
Though we have to go down deep into the mire.

This poem by Hannah Pope is a perfect example of the Pope sisters' evangelical Methodist piety and accompanying zeal for the Temperance Movement of the era. All of the passersby such as the "young maidens with curls like bright threads of gold" are admonished to roll up their sleeves and get their hands dirty.

28

URSULA VIRGINIA POPE

Working Girl ... Daughter of the Confederacy

"Do something for others
Something for others today!
Duty demands it, and Jesus commands it!
Do something for others today."

These lines from an old hymn book compiled by Homer Rodeheaver for use in evangelistic services by churches across the nation reflect the zeal embraced by both of John Michael Pope's daughters. Ursula Virginia, known as Miss Jennie, marked it in her copy as a favorite. She was extremely active in the Duncan Memorial Methodist Church, singing in the choir and, throughout her life, expressing a zeal for "service to others."

Miss Jennie, who was born in 1874, never married and seemed to be more worldly than her sister, Hannah. In 1898, at the age of 24, she applied for work at Coiner's Department Store as a sales lady. Several years later, according to E.G. Coiner himself (who wrote me in 1962), as the business grew a cash and carry system was put in place and Miss Jennie was made cashier and did the bookkeeping until 1922 when her health became bad and she had to retire.

Coiner's Department Store began operation in 1896 as the New York Racket Store at 24 East Main Street. "During the 1920s two grocery stores were brought here by horse pulled wagon and attached to the original structure ... A third floor was built and a new roof added over all three buildings." [1] Coiner's was the quintessential American department store, complete with pot bellied stove, and sold everything from sewing patterns to furniture, carpet, rugs and hardware.

There were few opportunities for women to work outside the home both in Berryville and across the nation and Miss Jennie was fortunate to not only find employment but also a position that gave her a sense of prominence in the community. Most people in town knew her well.

Miss Jennie became committed to "The Lost Cause" and, on January 16, 1897, was one of the founding members of a chapter of the United Daughters of the Confederacy. Its purpose was to "collect and preserve material for a truthful history of the war between the states, to protect historic places in the South and to aid in any way possible needy Confederate veterans and those dependent on them."

Appropriately, the Berryville chapter was named the Stonewall Chapter and supported fully the J.E.B. Stuart Camp of veterans to which Jennie's father belonged. The Stonewall Chapter was especially committed to having "true histories" used in schools believing "that in a great many instances wrong and harmful impressions have been made upon the minds of the youth of our country by the use of histories that were unfair to the South and the men who fought for the southern cause." [2] The Stonewall Chapter also took an active part in raising funds for the erection and overseeing the dedication of the Confederate monument standing in the courthouse square that can still be seen today.

Both the Daughters of the Confederacy and the J.E.B. Stuart Camp were political in nature. So much so that at one point Colonel Mosby, writing from the Department of Justice in Washington D.C., protested "they are political conventions in the guise of social gatherings. Nobody enjoys a talk over the old days more than I do, but I can't stand the speeches and prayers that are made … I prefer healing the wounds of war; I do not enjoy making them bleed afresh …" [3]

Jennie Pope was very much a daughter of the Confederacy and surely her legacy helped fire family remembrances and emotion in those 1950s New Haven days.

Ursula Virginia Pope
Photo the gift of E. G. Coiner to the author.

Coiner's Department Store.
Photograph by Virginia Pope.

Interior of Coiner's Department Store as Virginia Pope might have known it.
Photo courtesy of Clarke County Historical Association.

29

Arthur Townsend Pope

My grandfather, Arthur Townsend Pope, was born at Berryville in 1883. His middle name is for S. Townsend who served the Duncan Memorial Methodist Church from 1886 – 1889. Not very much is known of his life there or why, in his early 20s, he moved to New Haven, Connecticut. During his first years in New Haven he worked in sales for Gilbert's New England Bakery and it might have been that, given the predominance of its flour mills, Berryville was considered by northern bakeries as a good place to advertise employment opportunities.

Arthur is known through anecdotal stories as having been reserved towards the Methodist piety of his parents and sisters. One such story describes the family's attendance at a Sunday evening service at Duncan Memorial. At the conclusion of that service the minister exhorted all those who considered themselves "good Christians" to demonstrate their righteousness by coming forward to the altar. The entire congregation came forward with the exception of one – Arthur Pope. Hannah and Jennie fumed all the way home down Main Street about the ruination of the family brought about by Arthur's actions (or in this case inaction.) "How could you?!" they exclaimed to Arthur's feeble attempt to explain that, while he tried to strive toward the Methodist concept of Christian perfection, he had not yet arrived at the point where he could proclaim that he was a "good" Christian. By 1921, Arthur had fully embraced Christian Science. His surviving copy of *Science and Health with Key to the Scriptures* by Mary Baker Eddy is dogeared and voluminously annotated.

Soon after coming to New Haven he meets at a dance and later marries the strong-willed Minnie Fields who has a heritage that goes back to the early days of New Haven as well as to Plymouth, Massachusetts. They have four children: Ruth Esther (1909 – 1915), Lillian Virginia "Dixie" (1911 – 1917), Arthur Townsend, Jr. and my father, Warren Lee (1918 - 1991).

It was Arthur, Sr. who conveyed the great love of his parents and Berryville to his wife and children capturing their imaginations in such a way as to compel them to strongly convey the heritage to us, his grandchildren.

Minnie Fields Pope of New Haven (1886-1972) From old New Haven and Massachusetts families, she was known as a strong willed woman who, as a young girl, could not be hypnotized at a party in New Haven's Wooster Square. She visited Berryville once and learned to love it as strongly as her husband Arthur.

Arthur Townshend Pope as a young boy at Berryville. His health was never good and all his life he was a bit reclusive.

Arthur Townshend Pope loved all sports. He coached "sandlot" teams in New Haven and is shown here in the Bassett Junior High field. Always in coat and tie, always the southern gentleman, he is second from the right in the second row. Third in and next to him is his son Arthur, Jr. Second from the left in the first row is Warren Lee Pope, his youngest son and the author's father.

Ruth Esther and Lillian Virginia "Dixie" Pope

Minnie and Arthur had two daughters both of whom died under tragic circumstances at the age of 6. Ruth Esther died July 5, 1915 one day after a rocket in a fireworks exposition on the New Haven Green misfired and exploded in the crowd killing her and injuring a number of other children. Lillian Virigina "Dixie" died during the Great Flu Pandemic of 1918-1919.

**Virginia Pope with Nephews
Arthur Townshend Jr. and Warren Lee**

30

AT HOME IN BERRYVILLE

As the years pass, the town of Berryville continues to grow and prosper. By the 1880s, the national economy boomed and Berryville followed suit. The Berryville Building Association was even planning a resort hotel near a new train depot and a large park. During the first quarter of the 20th century electricity, telephones and the automobile arrive. Thomas Gold, Clarke County historian, was predicting that those "now living may see it [Berryville] grow into a city." [1]

John Michael Pope continues to be active with his fellow veterans and, during the last year of his life, is one of the founding members of the J.E.B. Stuart Camp of Confederate Veterans organized August 12, 1891. (Major General James Ewell Brown Stuart, a formidable southern morale booster, had been the trusted eyes and ears of Robert E. Lee's army.) The Camp was established to preserve local history connected with the war and to provide material aid to Confederate veterans. The very last meeting of the Camp for the year 1891 was to attend John Michael's funeral in late December. As we have seen, Virginia Pope took up the task of keeping alive this work and the spirit of the lost cause well into the 1920s.

John Michael's wife, Harriet, lived another 16 years after her husband's death, maintaining the home on West Main Street and bringing up her children. She engaged in what appears to have been a very successful business as a seamstress attested to by her designs that appear in photographs of her daughters and friends at Berryville. In a 1962 letter written to me, Mrs. Hugh G. Owens (Edna) remembers Harriet as a "very pretty, kind and fine looking old time lady with lovely white hair."

Harriet's obituary implies that her health was not good – "a sufferer for years" – and her death a difficult one. Her obituary states that "her sufferings were intense for a number of months. She knew her illness was incurable but she bore those sufferings bravely, patiently and with Christian fortitude."

The family had close friends in Berryville whose photographs survive in the family album. They bear the names of many families, some of whom I have met and are still living in the region today: Hardesty, Sponseller, Moore, Coiner, Cameron, Hart and Enders to name a few.

Prototypes of these friends are surely people like Province and Bessie McCormick. Bessie McCormick's photograph, as we have seen, was amongst the most fascinating of those found in the trunk in the attic in New Haven. In 1961 she was identified merely as "Mrs. Province McCormick, wife of the Indian Inspector." Many years later, as I have previously related, I met her grandson at Jane's Lunch and learned a bit more, but it was not until I was near the end of my journey of discovery that their story more fully unfolded.

The McCormick name goes deep into Irish and Virginian history. They were one of the slave owning families that played a role in the formation of Clarke County and in the Civil War. Province McCormick, Jr. was born February 18, 1847, attended the Academy at Berryville and, by the age of 16, was a courier at the headquarters of General Ewell and later the cavalry. He took part in the last fight with Lee just before the surrender. He entered the University of Virginia to study law but ill health forced him to turn to an "outdoor life" recommended by his physician and he became one of the progressive successful agriculturalists of Clarke County.

Under the second administration of President Cleveland, McCormick was appointed an Inspector in the Indian Service visiting just about every Indian reservation in the country. At home in Berryville, he established a room of Indian artifacts. Hence Bessie's photograph adorned with the same.

On December 6, 1871 he married Miss Elizabeth (Bessie) T. McCormick (a distant cousin), the only child of William and Sarah (Neal) McCormick. Orphaned early, she was raised by her grandmother. Province and Bessie had two children, Annis who married a Methodist minister, John B. Henry of Fairfax County, and Elizabeth T. who married Herbert Whiting who was engaged in the grain, coal and fertilizer business at Berryville. The Whitings had one child, Richard "Bev" Whiting, a charming southern gentleman who still lives in Berryville today and is the grandson I met in Jane's Lunch.

It was a long way home through the years from that trunk in the attic in New Haven for Bessie McCormick.

The McCormicks were typical of the families who were fairly close friends with the Popes in Berryville during the first quarter of the 20th century. In addition to their many friends, family continued to play a role in their lives especially with Michael and Conrad out towards Arabia and Stone's Chapel and, to a lesser extent, with Kilian at Winchester.

Michael and Elizabeth Swartz bore 14 children. Edward, born March 12, 1867, married Eva Belle McFillen and became a successful farmer in the Stone's Chapel area (Three Oaks Farm) as well as an active layman in the Crums Memorial Methodist Church. Many of their eight children and their offspring live in the region today and their contributions to life in Berryville were and continue to be legion.

It was interesting to discover that not all of the Popes were Methodist saints. A notation within the Annals of Clarke County describes the house of a well known Berryville

Constable, John Grubs and reads "He once went out to Arabia to serve a warrant on a lady named Pope and got shot in the backside (with a gunshot) … he could handle any man in the County but not the lady named Pope." [2] Fortunately, we do not know exactly who this certain relative was or what the infraction was that prompted the warrant.

After the deaths of their parents and George Cunningham, Hannah and Jennie continued to live full and rich lives at Berryville until May of 1931. At that time, having become frail, they were able to reap some rewards of their Methodism and entered the Asbury Methodist Home in Gaithersburg, Maryland.

In 1972, Esther Hart recalled the auction of their household including John Michael's tailor's goose. Typical of their Methodist faith, they received gifts such as the booklet presented to them by Mrs. A. Moore entitled "Prayer for Missions" and inscribed: "I shall sadly and fondly miss you, but hope to meet again in this world and the next." It surely must have been a sad day but, from all evidence, their lives at the Methodist Home were rich. They had many friends and continued to celebrate the faith that had sustained them all their lives. They died three months apart in December of 1936 and March of 1937 and were brought home to rest with their parents and Esther Lee at the Greenhill Cemetery in Berryville.

Shortly thereafter, their personal effects were shipped in a trunk to their brother Arthur in New Haven, Connecticut where it became a mysterious time capsule that, accompanied by oral history, illuminated their lives, the town of Berryville and Clarke County, Virginia, searing their memories into our hearts and minds.

Pope Family Homestead, West Main Street, Berryville
Photographed circa late 1950s by Arthur T. Pope, Jr.
when he and his wife, Val, visited Berryville for the first time.

Friendly Bible Class 1928 - Duncan Memorial Church
Front row far left Hannah Pope, third from left Virginia Pope three years
before they left Berryville. Hannah would have been 56, Virginia 54.

AT HOME IN BERRYVILLE | 99

Province McCormick holding grandson, Bev Whiting.
Bessie McCormick (insert)

IN MEMORIUM

After an illness of two weeks, Mrs. Hannah Pope Cunningham passed from "Our Home" at Gaithersburg, Md., to her Heavenly Home, on December 28, 1936.

> "They are not dead, those loved ones
> who have passed
> Beyond our vision for a little while.
> They have but reached the Light while
> we still grope
> In darkness where we cannot see them
> smile.
>
> "But smile they do, and love us, and
> do not
> Forget, nor ever go so far away
> But that their hands still clasp our
> hands and hold
> Us safe from falling when we fain
> would stray.

"They are not dead. Theirs is the fuller
life,
Theirs is the victory, the joy, the gain;
For us is still the waiting and the strife
For us the loneliness, for us the pain.

"Then let us gird us once again with
hope,
And give them smile for smile the
while we wait;
And loving, serving, when Our Father
calls,
We'll go to find our dear ones wait us
at the gate."

Her Sister,
Virginia Pope
The Home, Gaithersburg, Md.

Published in *The Baltimore Southern Methodist*

31

WHATEVER BECAME OF THE LOST CAUSE?

<u>Salute to the Confederate Flag</u>
"I salute the Confederate flag with affection, reverence and undying devotion to the Cause for which it stands."

<u>Salute to the Virginia Flag</u>
"I salute the flag of Virginia with reverence and patriotic devotion to the 'Mother of states and statesmen' which it represents – the 'Old Dominion', where liberty and independence were born."

Mrs. T.E. Gravely, United Daughters of the Confederacy

About 2012, I reached the point where my discovery was complete and the full story of family legend and emotions and the contents of the trunk in the attic in New Haven had come full circle. Yet there remained some final questions: What became of the great themes that dominated that discovery? How did the Lost Cause and Jim Crow/apartheid progress to the present day? These themes, after all, were an important part of my heritage, not to mention the heritage of Clarke County and of our country itself.

Over the years, when I tried to discover what happened to these concepts and ideals, I found that most people, natives and newcomers alike, knew little about them. Most popular modern histories of Clarke County, with one or two exceptions, are photographic essays or brief and anecdotal narratives that do not go into any depth on the topics.

This is not unusual as recent studies have revealed that many Americans have had their history reduced by the media to cartoon versions not unlike what I was subjected to in Grammar School. Abraham Lincoln once said "My fellow citizens, we cannot escape history." Often times today I think we have, simply by forgetting it.

With regard to the questions of slavery and race, this may, in part, have to do with the fact that blacks who once dominated the Clarke County region now number only in the hundreds. It is easy for the races to live separate lives and to be somewhat oblivious to each other as they have done for generations.

I have sensed that, throughout our society, underneath it all resentments and racism are still alive, and I feel I need to bring this part of my heritage to date because afterward, to paraphrase British abolitionist William Wilberforce, we can choose to look the other way, but we can never say again we did not know.

In 1973 I was struck by the grave of Mammy Emily Early not far from our family grave site in Green Hill Cemetery and it raised many questions in my mind. Little did I know at the time what that grave would reveal about the heritage of Berryville and Clarke County. Mammy Early of course represented the gilded cage of slavery, of the antebellum Dixie depicted in novels of the early 1900s as a genteel land of benevolent "planters" and happy "servants." A gilded cage perhaps, but, nevertheless, a cage.

The United Daughters of the Confederacy (UDC) of which Virginia Pope was a founding member in Berryville, sought to recast the "Lost Cause" as a noble defense of a southern utopia with Mammy representing the paternalism and affection between the races. Virginia Pope's ladies of the UDC honored aged blacks as "faithful confederates" and even ghost wrote testimonials such as "What Mammy Thinks of Freedom" in which an ex-slave says "Wen I gits ter hebben Lord, I hope I'll find it's slaberry."

In 1917, Annie C. Moore, writing in the Episcopal Church Missions Magazine, details her efforts to assist in the establishment of Saint Mary's Memorial Church in Berryville as a memorial to these colored mammies who "were faithful unto death to their white charges and to the service of women and men who owned their bodies." Ms. Moore, a good friend of Virginia Pope and fellow founding member of the UDC at Berryville, laments in her article "God grant that the negroes of today may prove themselves worthy of such noble ancestors, a type that the world can never see again, a people to be no more." [1]

In 1923, the national UDC had Charles Stedman, a North Carolina congressman, introduce a Mammy monument bill on its behalf. One sculpture model showed an Aunt Jemima like figure holding a white child as two other children clung to her dress. These were "pickaninnies," the artist explained, trying to have their mother pay attention to them instead of devoting all of her time to the white children. Stedman claimed of the slaves who were left that they looked back at those days as the happy golden hours of their lives. The Senate voted a land grant for the statue on the Washington Mall just weeks after it allowed a southern filibuster to defeat an anti lynching bill. Lynching had claimed some 2,500 lives between 1890 and 1920. The Chicago Defender published a cartoon titled "Mockery" in which a southerner presents plans for the Mammy statue to the dangling body of a lynching victim.

But the monument bill had to pass a House Committee before it could be enacted and it was allowed to die after black Americans organized a huge protest of letters and petitions.

Among these was a petition signed by 2,000 black women and presented to Vice President Calvin Coolidge. [2] The woman's auxiliary of the Grand Army of the Republic (Union veterans) condemned the monument as a sickly sentimental proposition and suggested the money could be better spent on bettering the conditions of Mammy's children.

The United Daughters of the Confederacy survived such set backs, however, and today remains an active organization in Virginia and throughout the South. It is the oldest patriotic organization in the country and remains committed, as it was in earlier times, to collecting and preserving materials for what they believe to be a truthful history of the war between the states, honoring the memory of those who fell in service by creating and preserving memorials to them. They also elevate the role of southern women's hardship during the war as well as their untiring efforts during the post war reconstruction of the South. The group offers scholarships for descendants of Confederates and cherishes the ties of friendship among its members.

As we have seen, the J.E.B. Stuart Camp of Confederate Veterans had been organized in Berryville in 1891 and grew out of the United Confederate Veterans (UCV) movement, in which John Michael had long been active. This movement was spurred on a couple of years later by "The Confederate Veteran" that, with a circulation of 20,000 readers, became one of the most popular magazines published in the South. The UCV's chief interest was in the field of history and it preserved the Confederate heritage, especially celebration of the average infantryman. It was believed that no concerted action had yet been taken to write their history except by those who were antagonistic to them.

In a 1906 address to the Sons of Confederate Veterans (SCV) Stephen Dill Lee charged them with "the defense of the Confederate soldier's good name, the guardianship of his history; the emulation of his virtues, the perpetuation of those principles he loved and which made him glorious." [3]

By the 1920s most of the work of the SCV was turned over to the Sons and Daughters of the Confederacy.

The Lost Cause is very much alive today as exemplified by such contemporary scholars within the Sons of the Confederacy as Edwin Ray. He holds that "the cause for which our grandfathers fought was the same one their grandfathers fought for, i.e., independence under constitutional, local government; it wasn't the right to keep slaves, it was the right to decide for themselves how to end slavery. Because our Confederate grandfathers were eventually 'compelled to yield to overwhelming numbers and resources' the South is understandably seen as having lost the war, and that our Cause was lost along with it. But I submit that all Americans suffered loss from that war; by which I mean that all Americans have suffered, whether they realize it or not, from the trampling of the constitution by Mr. Lincoln's authoritarian administration, the accumulation of power, then and since, by the central government in Washington, and the resulting incremental losses of freedom. We must not allow the Cause to be lost more than it has already lest we all become political slaves and the best form of government the world has known since Eden vanishes from the face of the earth." [4]

The Sons of Confederate Veterans (SCV) is active today in Virginia and throughout the South and continues to promote the preservation of Confederate history through museums and battlefields and scholarship that upholds their principles.

In recent years there has been activity on the part of some members of the SCV that moves towards the ideas of racist groups such as the League of the South and the Council of Conservative Citizens in much the same way that neo-Nazis and other hate groups proclaim their messages under the banner of the Confederate flag.

The way in which my forebears heard the cry of their times and gave their all to it is very clear to me. I agree that my great-grandfather did not fight for slavery but for the truths that the SCV continues to uphold: love of God and country, state sovereignty, regional duty, group solidarity and the protection of home and family.

But it can never be denied that "property rights" and "our way of life" included the enslavement and denial of basic civil rights to thousands of human beings, and that, unfortunately, the banner of the Lost Cause is today being distorted in ways far beyond what my family could have ever envisioned.

One thing that is for certain in all of this is that family members still living in Berryville and most of the folk who I met and talked with are, like John Mosby after the Civil War, thoroughly patriotic, thoroughly American and have proudly served our united nation in war and peace. The Confederacy is something in the past, limited to recalled moments of emotional indulgence not unlike those I experienced early on in New Haven and in the writing of this book.

Confederate Veterans Reunion at the Ammi Moore House c. 1885 – 1900. Identification of the veterans has not survived but most likely John Michael Pope is in this picture.

Photograph courtesy of Clarke County Historical Association

32

THE END OF JIM CROW

"The past is where the shaping of individuals and cultures and societies took place, is where many of the most revealing clues to the present and future are found"
       David Maraniss, *Barack Obama: The Story*

"The American conviction that one part of humanity was superior to another had led the culture of Berryville to support a repressive climate."
       Rennie Davis Chairman, Foundation for Humanity

As we have seen, after the Civil War African Americans were allowed to experience civil rights on a broad scale, including in Virginia, a constitutionally guaranteed statewide system of free state funded schools (non-integrated) for blacks and whites and voting rights for black men.

In 1877, following a contentious election, republican Rutherford B. Hayes was declared President. In order to gain the votes he needed from southern democrats who called themselves "the Redeemers" he agreed to pull federal troops out of the south, thus ending reconstruction. The Redeemers were a white ruling class who took control of southern state legislators and stripped African Americans of many of their gained rights. Cultural prejudice in the south became a matter of law in a very short time.

A new constitution in Virginia (1902) created the climate that kept the races in towns like Berryville apart in every area of life. "Black children could not enter a library and check out a book. Loopholes were written into (this) constitution which were deliberately designed to withhold funds from black schools denying black children an equal education. Voting laws were designed to make it nearly impossible to cast a ballot. Poll taxes, literacy tests and intimidation were allowed tactics for policemen and sheriffs ... This was (the) law (!)" [1]

This was the climate in which the John Michael Pope family lived into the 1930s. Until the passage of the Civil Rights Act of the 1960s there was not much change. When the Supreme Court ordered school integration in 1954, Berryville native U.S. Senator Harry

F. Byrd, Sr., who controlled Virginia politics, called the decision a "usurpation of power" by the Court and promoted the "Southern Manifesto" opposing integrated schools. The Manifesto was signed in 1956 by more than 100 southern office holders. "On February 25, 1956, Byrd called for what became known as Massive Resistance. This was a group of laws passed in 1958 and intending to prevent integration of the schools. Placement Boards were created with the power to assign specific students to particular schools. Tuition grants were to be provided to students who opposed integrated schools. The linchpin of Massive Resistance was a law that cut off funds and closed any public schools that agreed to integrate." [2]

Despite the fact that these laws were repealed by the General Assembly of Virginia and a Federal Court verdict based on the Equal Protection Clause of the 14th Amendment, with the exception of a few courageous black students in the state, hardly any black students in Virginia attended integrated schools.

In 1982, Byrd's son, Harry Byrd, Jr., told the Washington Post that he "personally hated" to see the schools close but even these many years later he didn't disavow Massive Resistance and suggested it helped the state avoid racial violence. He said "When you have to make a very dramatic change, sometimes, most times that needs to be done maybe over a period of time and not abruptly." [3]

My journey of discovery led me to Rennard (Rennie) Davis, a world citizen who spent his formative years growing up during the 1950s (about the same time I was discovering my southern heritage) on a 500-acre farm, "Morgan's Mill," two miles outside of Berryville. After graduating as valedictorian of Clarke County High School, Davis went on to become a leader during the anti-Vietnam war movement helping to organize massive civil disobedience demonstrations including protests with Tom Hayden at the 1968 Democratic National Convention. He was indicted as one of the Chicago 7 and was a principal figure in what the New York Times has called the "most significant political trial in U.S. history." Davis went on to become a venture capitalist, lecturer on meditation and self awareness, and founder of the Foundation for Humanity. [4] All of this indeed a long way from Berryville.

Berryville, however, is still the place Davis calls his hometown and his nostalgic memories of the place strikingly parallel the discoveries of this book. Davis talks fondly of this area of the Blue Ridge Mountains and calls them majestic monuments amidst a world of lush nature. He proudly talks about meeting John Denver and calculates that his song "Country Road" was actually based on the area. His family farm, Morgan's Mill, was a working sheep and chicken farm with "6,000 boilers on the fast track." The farm was purchased by Davis' father, John C. Davis, who moved to the Valley after he had served as President Harry Truman's chief of staff of the Council of Economic Advisers. He also owned and operated the Berryville Feed Store.

Today Davis remembers the same Berryville that I have written about. He remembers Main Street fondly and so many of the personages who dominated life there in the 1950s. He talks about the drugstore on Main Street, Jane's Lunch, attending Duncan Memorial Methodist Church, and can give enthusiastic descriptions of Coiner's Department Store.

Davis related to me that, like most of his contemporaries, he was unaware growing up in Clarke County of the great racial divide that dominated the area. His only contact with blacks was with the Potter brothers who operated a barber shop on Main Street. He says that the black community was invisible to him. Davis speaks about his high school being all white and that he never thought much of how that came to be. He says that in 1958, the year he gave the valedictorian address at Clarke County High School, it never crossed his mind that racism was truly the main issue facing the future of his class.

Davis concludes, as I do, that it has taken many years since the 1950s for the people of Clarke County and Americans everywhere to begin the great work to bring an end to this underground river of the dark natures of ourselves. It may well be possible that for some things are still the same as they were in Davis' or John Michael Pope's time. It is interesting to note, however, that children in Clarke County schools and throughout the country will never again be unaware of Jim Crow given the development of school curricula that objectively present its history.[5]

33

GOING HOME, AGAIN AND AGAIN

"Hold on to the now, the here through which all of the future plunges to the past."

James Joyce, Ulysses

In the 1970s, under pressure from the post World War II housing boom with its residential subdivisions, Clarke County developed a comprehensive plan focused on its land based heritage of a "separate place and a rural jewel" resulting in more than 20% of the county being in permanent conservation easement and over 30% of the county divided into three rural historic districts dominated by horse farms with some 500 historic structures.[1] Likewise, the town of Berryville, now on the doorstep of the suburbs of Washington DC, has been able to keep its historic character and rural charm. In 1988 the Berryville historic district was listed in the National Register and the town became a designated Virginia Main Street community in 1992. Since then some 200 buildings have been rehabilitated.

All of this makes it quite possible for everyone with a heritage in this American place to experience it again and again, for here the air is hallowed by the breath of other times. In terms of my own heritage, every time I return, those strange, wonderful feelings of genetic memory re-emerge.

I can go out to Stone's Chapel and stand in the environment in which Johannes Popp, as well as several other family members, lived and are buried and can gaze upon a landscape that is not so very much different than that experienced by Johannes and his children. I can meet descendants out towards Arabia of the very same people that he and the rest of our family knew as reasonably close friends.

I shall never forget, for example, the bright summer day that Larry Hardesty, whose forebears were friends of my ancestors, showed my wife Esther, my cousin Lois Marbert and me all over that area in rich fellowship not unlike the two families experienced a century and a half ago.[2] Larry is President of the Stone's Chapel Memorial Association dedicated to preserving and maintaining the chapel and cemetery and to educating the citizens of Clarke County and the general public about its relationship to the rich history and diverse communities of Clarke County.[3]

Visitors like myself can still go out into the fields of one of the great surviving plantations and, if very still, can hear the songs of hundreds of slaves yet wafting upon the air. Although only a few of their descendants remain in the area, we can reflect on how in the thousands, for over 200 years, they have made a faith-based recovery from so many of the ills that plagued them.

We can visit the intact, but somewhat declined, black community of Josephine City now incorporated into the town of Berryville. In 1882, the former slaves and free colored built Josephine City School to provide a segregated grade school education and, in 1930, the Clarke County Training School to provide a high school education. The original Josephine City School, now on the National Register of Historic Places, is today a museum devoted to the history of Clarke County's African Americans. [4] A visit there, meeting folks along the streets of the community and attending worship at Zion Baptist Church are educational and inspiring experiences. Josephine City itself has recently been placed on the National Register of Historic Places.

Everyone can visit the Burwell-Morgan Flour Mill at Millwood now owned and operated by the Clarke County Historical Association. An imposing water powered Merchant Mill dating to 1785, it not only tells the story of how Berryville and Clarke County thrived on the corn and wheat that was sent to European markets, but also the stories of its builders. They were Brigadier General Daniel Morgan who contributed to Berryville's first name, Battletown, and Lt. Colonel Nathaniel Burwell of Carter's Grove Plantation near Williamsburg, a member of one of Virginia's oldest families and owner of Carter Hall, one of the great manor homes of Virginia which still stands nearby. Burwell owned 175 slaves here. [5]

Revisiting the Civil War in Clarke County, we can return again and again to all of its scenes. We can go north to Harpers Ferry and its National Historical Park where the sites of this quaint historic community become as alive as they were in the 19th century. [6]

Interpretive guides to all of the Civil War battle sites and monuments abound as they do for the heritage of Colonel John Mosby. John Michael Pope's Stonewall Brigade lives on in a modern day reenactment group. [7]

Best of all, we can visit Berryville (pop. 4,000) and its Main Street that really hasn't changed all that much in 150 years! You can stop by Jane's Lunch and most likely run into several of the people mentioned in this book or perhaps one of their descendants. The Clarke County Historical Association can be visited to experience in more depth all of the history detailed in this book. The museum is located in the former home of E.G. Coiner whose department store building still stands renovated, preserved and vacant, awaiting a tenant for these modern times. [8]

From there it is an easy walk back up to the historic corner of Buckmarsh and Main. The Showers House where John Michael grew up still stands and, until recently, it operated as the Battletown Inn. Like Coiner's Department Store, it is vacant, a ghost of its former self awaiting some 21st century reuse. From there you can walk up Church Street to the still used restored Courthouse, the Episcopal Church, the Confederate Monument erected by Virginia Pope's Daughters of the Confederacy, and the granite marker where Robert E. Lee tethered his horse, Traveler, during his Civil War visit to Berryville.

An emotional spot is the Green Hill Cemetery where the John Michael Pope family and their friends lie buried. John Michael's Confederate marker is rusted and unceremoniously propped in the ground and inscriptions on all of the tilted stones have faded. Emily "Mammy" Early's lichen and moss covered stone is obscured and hidden amid brush and pine and hard to find.

Some things you cannot readily find. You won't see many Confederate flags or other remnants of the lost cause. Its Evangelical Christian faith does remain strong, but it carries some modern day heavy conservative political baggage and has, in part, morphed into what we know as the religious right.

The structure of the Duncan Memorial Methodist Church that the family knew has been replaced by one of 20th century generic design that shelters a large congregation that holds forth with a traditional vision of worship and service. I do believe that Hannah and Jennie would feel quite comfortable there.

Lee Child in his Jack Reacher novel *Never Go Back* has his main character walking through Berryville "on a street called West Main." He writes "All the doors were shuttered. Berryville was no doubt a fine American town, matter of fact and unpretentious, but it was no kind of a hub that was for damn sure. It was all closed up and slumbering even though it was the middle of the evening." [9]

But I can sit at a window seat at another site mentioned in Child's novel – the Berryville Grill – and look at local life passing by and proclaim exactly the opposite. Berryville, Virginia is a mighty hub. It is the hub of American immigration and assimilation, of America's natural and built environment, of American small town family life and tradition.

It is in Berryville that you can study American religious experience, black history, the American Civil War, the modern day preservation movement and the struggle of modern American small towns as they confront not only their past but urban sprawl and the socio-economic forces that have and continue to threaten them.

Over the years, as I have been carried back to Berryville one thing has become very clear to me. It is that each of us has a heritage and a story to tell. If I have accomplished one thing here, I hope it is to inspire others to let their own family legends and stories carry them back. May others be inspired to take their own enriching journey in time and place to the enclosures of the past, to discover or rediscover how their own unique heritage parallels our rich American story. That, I again submit, can be one of the most enriching and enlightening experiences that life has to offer.

The still used Clarke County Courthouse remains as it was when it was built.
Photo courtesy of Jon Bridgan,
Focus on the Valley Photography, Berryville, VA

Coiner's Department store today.

Surviving early home in Josephine City.

Former Battletown Inn where J.M. Pope spent formative years.

Esther Pope photos.

Afterword

There are places I remember
All my life though some have changed
Some forever not for better
Some have gone and some remain …

In My Life
The Beatles

In the "made for television" movie *Welcome Home Johnny Bristol*[1], an American service man is released from a Vietnamese prisoner of war camp and comes home with the goal of finding his original home. He has been so brainwashed through torture that he has few memories of his life before prison.

At first, the only thing he can remember is that he was born and raised in the idyllic small town of Charles, Vermont. The problem is that, after investigation and trips to Vermont to find his boyhood home and family, he discovers that there is no Charles, Vermont!

Finally, Johnny traces his heritage to a decayed section of a northeastern city far from idyllic, romantic Vermont and is able to locate his childhood home. The movie's Rod Serling-like ending finds him gazing up at a street sign on the corner of Charles Street and Vermont Avenue in Philadelphia, Pennsylvania!

This book began in the Newhallville section of New Haven, Connecticut, in the 1950s. If one were to attempt to find that neighborhood today as I described it, the quest might prove as illusive as finding Johnny Bristol's Charles, Vermont. My memories of the neighborhood, however, are not false, confused or overly romanticized. It is simply that, unlike Berryville, Virginia, until recently I could not go home again, so drastic were the changes in terms of landscape, tradition and people. By 1980, the Federal census found New Haven to be the 7th poorest city in America. Almost unbelievably, over the course of 50 years, the Newhallville of my youth became one of the poorest, most dangerous, gang and drug abuse ridden areas in Connecticut. It is still scorned by the media and many former residents.

Unlike Berryville, where I can yet walk the streets to conjure up memories of the past, until recent years I was warned that it was not safe to walk my old neighborhood streets, even in broad daylight! Unemployment, poverty, boredom, racism and fear, New Haven's sometimes failed urban renewal program, gangs and a multimillion dollar cocaine industry took the old neighborhood away. The six o'clock news on television still today echoes New Haven's and Newhallville's high crime rate once greater than that of Washington, Detroit, Dallas and New York.

Like Johnny Bristol, what I sought could not be found. In place of Farnam's Farm, its lagoon, dirt roads and all of the places where we celebrated our childhood pastimes of sledding, hiking, building forts, playing baseball and even trapping muskrats for pelts, West Rock now looks down upon the sprawling steel and glass campus of Southern Connecticut State University with traffic throughout the area increased a hundred fold.

Within 20 years of my earlier narrative, the Newhall Street small town business district, supported by the Winchester Repeating Arms Factory with its at one time 6,000 employees, dry goods stores, barber shops, dentist and meat market, had completely vanished. Blight, crime and despair were everywhere. "There was a shooting darn near every night." [2] Almost without exception, long time residents had fled to the suburbs and newcomers who once saw the area as the promised land had their hopes dashed as their homes became fortresses at night when the streets in the darkness were ruled by gangs. [3]

In the last few years, however, there has been another turn around in the neighborhood (as there has been in New Haven) and Newhallville has been placed on the National Register of Historic Places as an historic district. This may seem odd considering the neighborhood's recent history. Yet a combination of neighborhood residents, educators, private and government groups, and law enforcement have worked together resulting in the emergence of a new neighborhood. In some ways the new neighborhood, at least in terms of the human spirit, is not unlike the old. A good deal of the blight on its yet tree lined streets has been demolished and replaced with new housing that fits in well with the mostly remodeled and restored late 19th and early 20th century housing stock. The old railroad tracks and the remnants of the Farmington Canal have been developed as a serene greenway through New Haven to Long Island Sound.

On a recent, sunny June day, while walking down Newhall Street I stopped and engaged in a conversation with a long time resident enjoying her front porch. (My grandfather had owned the house next door many years ago.) Detailed memories sprung to life.

We shared many stories, especially about one of my maternal grandfather's tenants who had lived next door. She was a touring tent evangelist and stored her tent in my grandfather's garage. You can imagine my surprise at learning that the evangelist was still alive at the age of 104!

That same day, on a tour sponsored by the International Festival of Arts and Ideas and the New Haven Preservation Trust, I met a Newhallville native about my age. She and I spent a long time revisiting, in our hearts and minds, most of the commercial endeavors and many a family who had lived in the neighborhood in its idyllic days decades before.

Newhallville is reemerging as a desirable place to live. There may not be any history revealing trunks left in any attics, but I am very confident that the neighborhood will yet yield a wealth of memories that will contribute in a significant way to telling our American story.

Acknowledgments

The number of people who have had a role over the years in the production of this book is legion.

First and foremost, I would like to thank Wendy Knight who has served as my editorial assistant. Wendy rescued me from my less than stellar computer skills and her enthusiastic and heartfelt response to the people, places and events in my tale gave me great encouragement.

Early on in the book I acknowledge that family legend held that folks were friendlier *down south* and that has held true in my discovery of them. It would not have been possible to tell this story without the input of people like Esther Hart Enders, Dolly Enders, Nora Forester Hardesty and her daughter, Muriel Gregory, Larry Hardesty, all the folks at the Clarke County Historical Association, Bev Whiting, Gene Cunningham, several times removed cousins Lois Marbert and Cheyenne Cashin whose travels and superb genealogical research into the legacy of Johannes Popp helped me fill a lot of gaps, and countless business owners and citizens I have met along the way both in Clarke and adjoining counties.

Everyone who undertakes a project like this does so with a degree of insecurity, wondering if their story has any significance or appeal. My thanks to all those prolific souls who helped me realize I *was* really on to something. They include my friend and retired English professor, James Killian, my daughter-in-law, Este Paskausky Pope, who is an academic librarian, Shirley and Rudy Nelson, my college English professors and Colin Caplan, architect and New Haven historian.

Whether this book was to emerge as worthwhile or not, there is one person who has had to endure its progress and provide support and that is my wife, Esther. After all, this is not *her* family story. Yet she has been at my side through these many years of its developing and I do believe has also become fascinated by these people, living and dead, and has fondly taken them as her own. This is my greatest endorsement and the one that merits my most heartfelt thank you.

NOTES

Pre-Intro   Joan Didion, *The White Album* (Simon & Schuster, 1979).

Chapter 2   1. Tony Horwitz, *Confederates in the Attic* (New York: Vintage Books, 1999).

Chapter 3   1. Raymond Lane, "My Mother's Deep Green Secret" (*AARP The Magazine*, February/March 2013) 52-53.

Chapter 6   1. *Diary of Michael Friedrich Radke*

Chapter 7   1. *Diary of Michael Friedrich Radke*

Chapter 9   1. Thomas A. Lewis, *For King and Country*, (John Wiley & Sons, 1993) 27. Maps courtesy of Nancy Morbeck Haack, Purcellville, Virginia

Chapter 11   1. Curtis D. Johnson, *Redeeming America* (Chicago: Ivan R. Dee, Inc., 1993) 5.
2. *Ibid*, 7.
3. Thomas D. Gold, *History of Clarke County* (Forgotten Books, 2012) 102.
4. *Songs of Zion* (Nashville: Abington Press, 1981) IX.

Chapter 12   1. Jay Winik, *April 1865* (New York: Perennial/Harper Collins, 2002) 45.
2. Myers/Brown, *Notes on the Civil War from Treadwell Smith's Diary, Annals of Clarke Co. VA*, Vol. IV.
3. "John Brown's Raid at Harper's Ferry: An Eyewitness Account" (*The Virginia Magazine of History and Biography* 67) 387-395.
4. *Ibid*

Chapter 13　　1. Gold, 153.
　　　　　　　2. Kenneth C. Davis, *Don't Know Much About the Civil War* (Avon Books, 1997) 152.
　　　　　　　3. Gold, 153.

Chapter 14　　1. Hook/Smith, *The Stonewall Brigade in the Civil War* (Zenith Press, 2008) 121.
　　　　　　　2. Bell Irvin Wiley, *The Life of Johnny Reb* (Louisiana State University Press, 1943) 29.

Chapter 15　　1. Thomas Allen, *The Blue and The Gray* (National Geographic Society, 1992) 136.
　　　　　　　2. Drew Gilpin Faust, *The Creation of Confederate Nationalism* (Louisiana State University Press, 1988) 27.
　　　　　　　3. Wikipedia, Robert E. Lee, pg. 3

Chapter 16　　1. Wikipedia, Thomas "Stonewall" Jackson, pg.5

Chapter 17　　1. Hook/Smith, 53.

Chapter 18　　1. Gold, 180.
　　　　　　　2. Mark Summers, "The Great Harvest" (Acton Institute, *Religion and Liberty*, Vol. 21, No. 3).
　　　　　　　3. James I. Robertson, Jr., *Soldiers Blue and Gray* (University of South Carolina Press, 1988) 187.
　　　　　　　4. Wiley, 184.
　　　　　　　5. *Religion and Liberty*, Acton Institute

Chapter 19　　1. John Casler, *Four Years in the Stonewall Brigade* (Appeal Publishing Co., 1906, University of South Carolina Press, 2005).
　　　　　　　2. Davis, 292.
　　　　　　　3. John Casler
　　　　　　　4. Hook/Smith, 73.
　　　　　　　5. John Casler

Chapter 21　　1. National Park Service, August 21, 2006, U.S. Dept. of the Interior, Battle of Mine Run

2. J. Steven Wilkins, *Call of Duty, the Sterling Nobility of Robert E. Lee* (Nashville: Cumberland House Publishing, 1997).

Chapter 22   1. Robertson, 167.

Chapter 23   1. Winik, 303.
2. Gold, *History of Clarke County, Virginia*
3. Myers/Brown, *Annals of Clarke County* (Virginia Book Co., 1983, 2002) 288.
4. Myers/Brown, 7.
5. Winik, 64.
6. Mosbyheritagearea.org

Chapter 24   1. Winik, 33.
2. Myers/Brown, 11.
3. Winik, 353.
4. Gold, 223.
5. Richard K. Kolb, *Thin Gray Line* (www.vfw.org)

Chapter 25   1. Myers/Brown, 75.
2. Marie Hileman, *Slaves Left Their Mark on Clarke County, Winchester Star*, quote from Dorothy Davis, August 14, 2012
3. Carolyn Watts, curriculum, Cooley Elementary School, Clarke Co. Maral S. Kalbian, *Clarke County (Images of America)*, (Arcadia Publishing Co., 2011).
5. Gold, 101.

Chapter 26   1. Thornton Wilder, *Our Town: A Play in Three Acts* (Harper Rowe, 1938, 1957).

Chapter 28   1. *Berryville Celebrates*
2. Gold, pg. 320
3. *Berryville Celebrates* (Clarke County Historical Association, 1998) 139.

Chapter 30   1. Gold, 39.
2. Myers/Brown, 134.

Chapter 31   1. James F. Moore, *Forth*, Volume 82 (Google e Book, 1917 Missions).

2. Tony Horwitz, "The Mammy Washington Almost Had" (*The Atlantic*, May 31, 2013)
3. Stephen Dill, www.scvva.org
4. Edwin Ray, www.scvva.org

Chapter 32
1. Carolyn Watts
2. Virginia Historical Society Collection, "Civil Rights Massive Resistance"
3. Associated Press, July 30, 2013
4. http://ffh.org
5. Watts, "Resistance to Jim Crow in Virginia"

Chapter 33
1. Clarke County Conservation, *Our Land is Our Legacy*, Guidebook to Clarke County Historical Association Exhibit
2. Lois Marbert, my second cousin, descendant of Kilian Pope, has traced the Johannes Popp family back to Helmstadt, Germany. She has visited the town in modern times which now enjoys one of the highest standards of living in the world.
3. www.stoneschapel.org
4. www.Jschoolmuseum.org
5. www.clarkehistory, org
6. www.nps.gov/hafe/index.htm
7. www.stonewallbrigade.net
8. www.clarkehistory.org
9. Lee Child, *Never Go Back, A Jack Reacher Novel* (Delacorte Press/Random House, 2013).

Afterword
1. *Welcome Home Johnny Bristol* (1972)
2. Geoffrey Douglas, *Dead Opposite* (Henry Holt & Co., 1995)
3. *Ibid*

Selected Bibliography

Allen, Thomas. *The Blue and The Gray.* Book Division/National Geographic Society, 1992.

Allen, William Francis, Lucy McKim Garrison and Charles Pickard Ware. *Slave Songs of the United States (1867).* Bedford, MA: Applewood Books.

Casler, John O.. *Four Years in the Stonewall Brigade.* Appeal Publishing Company, 1906. (with new introduction, University of South Carolina Press, 2005)

Crocker III, H.W. *Robert E. Lee on Leadership.* Forum/Prima Publishing, 1999.

Davis, Kenneth C.. *Don't Know Much About the Civil War.* Avon Books, 1997.

Didion, Joan. *The White Album.* Simon & Schuster, 1979.

Douglas, Geoffrey. *Dead Opposite: The Lives and Loss of Two American Boys.* Henry Holt and Company, 1995.

Eisenberg, William Edward. *This Heritage – The Story of Lutheran Beginnings in the Lower Shenandoah Valley.* Carr Publishing, 1954.

Faust, Drew Gilpin. *The Creation of Confederate Nationalism.* Louisiana State University Press, 1988.

Freehling, William W. *The South vs The South.* New York: Oxford University Press Inc., 2001.

Gold, Thomas Daniel. *History of Clarke County, Virginia* (1914). Forgotten Books, 2012.

Harwell, Richard B. *The Confederate Reader – How the South Saw the Civil War.* Dorset Press, 1992.

Hofstra, Warren R. *A Separate Place.* Madison House Publishers, 1999.

Hook, Patrick and Steve Smith. *The Stonewall Brigade in the Civil War.* Zenith Press, 2008.

Horwitz, Tony. *Confederates in the Attic.* New York: Vintage Books, 1999.

Horwitz, Tony. *Midnight Rising – John Brown and the Raid that Sparked the Civil War.* Henry Holt, 2011.

Johnson, Curtis D. *Redeeming America: Evangelicals and the Road to Civil War.* Chicago: Ivan R. Dee, Inc., 1993.

Justin, Martin. *Genius of Place, The Life of Frederick Law Olmstead.* Da Capo Press/Perseus Books, 2011.

Kalbian, Maral S. *Clarke County (Images of America).* Arcadia Publishing Co., 2011.

Lewis, Thomas A. *For King and Country, George Washington the Early Years.* John Wiley & Sons, 1993.

Longenecker, Stephen L. *Shenandoah Religion: Outsiders and the Mainstream 1716-1865.* Waco, TX: Baylor University Press, 2002.

McCaig, Donald. *Jacob's Ladder: A Story of Virginia During the Civil War.* New York: W.W. Norton & Co., 1999.

Myers, Lorraine F. and Stuart E. Brown, Jr. *Annals of Clarke County, Virginia, Volume IV.* Virginia Book Company, June 1983, 2002.

Neely, Mark, Harold Holzer and Gabor Boritt. *The Confederate Image: Prints of a Lost Cause.* University of North Carolina Press, 1987.

Negri, Paul. *Civil War Poetry: An Anthology.* Dover Publications, 1997.

Pope, Arthur K. *The Heart Strangely Warmed.* Trafford Publishing, 2006.

Robertson, Jr., James. *Soldiers Blue and Grey.* University of South Carolina Press, 1988.

Rowe, Edward Payson, *Opening a Chestnut Burr.* New York: Dodd & Mead, 1874.

Summers, Mark. *The Great Harvest: Revival in the Confederate Army During the Civil War.* (*Religion & Liberty*, Volume 21, No. 3). Acton Institute.

Taylor, Elizabeth Dowling, *A Slave in the White House.* Palgrove, MacMillian, 2011.

Taylor, James E. *Sketchbook – With Sheridan up the Shenandoah Valley in 1864*, Western Reserve Historical Society.

Watts, Carolyn. *Resistance to Jim Crow in Virginia*, curriculum D.G.Cooley Elementary School, Clarke County.

Wilder, Thornton. *Our Town, a Play in Three Acts*, Harper Rowe, 1938, 1957.

Wiley, Bell Irvin. *The Life of Johnny Reb.* Louisiana State University Press, 1943.

Wilkins, J. Steven. *Call of Duty: The Sterling Nobility of Robert E. Lee.* Nashville, TN: Cumberland House Publishing, 1997.

Williamson, James J. *Mosby's Rangers.* New York: Ralph B. Kenyon Publisher, 1896.

Winik, Jay. *April 1865.* New York: Perennial (Harper Collins), 2002.

American Panorama: Portraits of 50 States by Distinguished Authors. A Holiday Marketplace Book. Doubleday & Co., Inc., 1960.

AARP The Magazine. Lane, Raymond. "My Mother's Deep Green Secret". February/March 2013.

Associated Press, "Former Senator Harry Byrd, Jr. of Virginia Dies", July 30, 2013.

The Atlantic, Horwitz, Tony. "The Mammy Washington Almost Had". May 31, 2013.

Berryville Celebrates. Clarke County Historical Association, 1998.

Forth, Volume 82 (Google e Book). James F. Moore, 1917 Missions.

Harper's Magazine

History of Virginia, Volume I, Part II Biography

John Brown's Raid at Harpers Ferry – an Eyewitness Account by Charles White, Ed. Rayburn S. Moore, The Virginia Magazine of History and Biography 67 (Oct. 1959: 387-395) (www2.lath, Virginia.edu/jbrown/umhb.html)

New York Tribune

Proceedings/Journal of the Clarke County Historical Association, Vol. XXVI, 2008.

Songs of Zion. Abington Press, Nashville, 1981.

Virginia Historical Society Collections and Resources, *The World of Jim Crow*.

Virginia Historical Society Historical Collections: Civil Rights Movement, *Massive Resistance*.

Winchester Evening Star, Hileman, Marie. "Slaves Left Their Mark on Clarke County". August 14, 2012.

www.exulanten.com

www.emslanders.com

www.myjewishlearning.com

www.teachers.ash.org

http://www.ingenweb.org/infranklin/pages/tier2/radke1848.html
Michael Fredrich Radke, 1848, *A German Immigration Diary*

SELECTED BIBLIOGRAPHY | 129

(footnote end of Chap 6)

www.provocate.org

www.auswander

www.secureancestry.com

http://wikipedia.org

www.ancestry.com

www.50states.com/songs/virginia

www.Mosbyheritagearea.org

Wikipedia.org/wiki/carry_me_back_to_old_virginny

Wikipedia, *The Bonnie Blue Flag*

www.acton.org/pub/religion-liberty/volume-21-number-3/great-harvest-revival-confederate-army-during-civil

http://vaudc.org/confed_vets.html
Veterans of Foreign Wars of the United States
Kolb, Richard, *Thin Grey Line*

http://www.nps.gov/nr/travel/vamainstreet/ber.htm
Clarke County Historical Assoc., *Our Land is our Legacy*, Guidebook to historical exhibit

http://www.yale.edu/ynhti/curriculum/units/1989/1/89.01.14.x.html
Smith, Carolyn, *Newhallville: A neighborhood of Changing Prosperity*, Yale New Haven Teachers Institute curriculum

www.scvv.org

en.wikisource.org/Century-Magazine
The Century Magazine (1881-1930)

www.stoneschapel.org

www.Jschoolmuseum.org

www.clarkehistory.org

www.nps.gov/hafe/index.htm

http://ffh.org

www.stonewallbrigade.net

Songs and Poems

Carry Me Back to Old Virginny

The Bonnie Blue Flag

Stonewall Jackson's Way

On Jordan's Stormy Banks

Tribute to the Confederate Soldiers, John O. Crown

Down in the Mire, Hannah Pope

In Memorium, Virginia Pope

About the Author

New Englander Arthur Pope has enjoyed multifaceted careers in the ministry, historic preservation and progressive social justice causes. An historian and journalist, he is the author of several books and numerous articles that have appeared in such publications as Yankee Magazine, Connecticut Explored, the New Haven (Ct.) Register and the New England Antiques Journal.